BEGINNING GUITARIST'S HANDBOOK

Publisher *David A. Lusterman*
Editors *Stacey Lynn and Simone Solondz*
Music Editor *Andrew DuBrock*
Designer *Trpti Todd*
Production *Christopher Maas*
Production Director *Ellen Richman*
Marketing *Jen Fujimoto*

Photographs: front cover (clockwise from top) by Barbara Gelfand, Christopher Maas, and Trpti Todd; pp. viii, 21, 26, 36, 44, 45, 46 (top), 54, 55, 56, 59, 60, 62, 65 (bottom), 71, 75, 76, 78, 82, 86, 94, Trpti Todd; pp. 3, 27, 38, 47, 50-53, 57, 66, 104, 116, Christopher Maas; pp. 5, 111, Anne Hamersky; pp. 7, 10, 80, 110, courtesy National Guitar Workshop; pp. 29, 34 (bottom), Paul Kotapish; pp. 12, 42, 46 (bottom), Scott Blum; p. 56, Gary Cribb; p. 62, Rory Earnshaw; pp. 67-69, 90-92, Andrew DuBrock; pp. 84, 108, Barbara Gelfand; p. 88, courtesy Sonia Michelson; p. 106, courtesy Interlochen Center for the Arts; p. 124, Cecilia Van Hollen

Contents © 2001 String Letter Publishing
Printed in the United States of America

Library of Congress Cataloging-in-Publication Data
Rodgers, Jeffrey Pepper, 1964-
    The beginning guitarist's handbook/by Jeffrey Pepper Rodgers.
    p. cm.
    ISBN 1-890490-45-8
    1. Guitar–Miscellanea. I. Title

    ML1015.G9 R59 2001
    787.87'19–dc21

BEGINNING GUITARIST'S HANDBOOK

JEFFREY PEPPER RODGERS

STRING LETTER PUBLISHING

CONTENTS

Introduction vi

ALL KINDS OF BEGINNERS

Guitar vs. other instruments 1
Different ages, different stages 2
Starting as a kid 4
Girl guitarists and the boys' club 5
"My family isn't musical" 7
Sibling rivalries 9
Beginning as an adult 9

GUITAR SHOPPING

Basic types of guitars 13
Acoustic vs. electric 20
Steel-string vs. classical 21
Acoustic vs. acoustic-electric 23
Kids' guitars 25
Lefty guitars 27
Renting and borrowing 28
Price range and quality 28
Finding the right fit 33
Routine adjustments and fatal flaws 35
Where to shop 37
Smart shopping 39

EQUIPMENT BASICS

Why you need a good setup 43
Essential accessories 45
Types and gauges of strings 47
Changing strings 49
Cases 53
Commonsense care 55
Picks and fingers 58
Using a capo 60

GETTING IN TUNE AND GETTING STARTED

How to tune 63

"I've got blisters on my fingers!" .69

Fingering problems 71

Smooth changes 73

Rhythm and lead 74

Flatpicking and fingerstyle 75

Tackling barre chords 76

Singing and playing 79

THE LEARNING PROCESS

Practicing secrets 81

Self-teaching vs. taking lessons 84

Choosing a teacher 85

Suzuki guitar 88

To read or not to read 89

Video instruction 93

Computer guitar lessons 94

Learning songs off records 96

Alternate tunings 99

Measuring progress 101

SHARING YOUR MUSIC

Overcoming shyness 105

Jamming with people 107

Music camps 109

Getting ready to perform 111

Staying inspired 113

Resources 117

Index of guitar lingo 121

About the author 124

Acknowledgments 125

INTRODUCTION

Learning to play the guitar is an incredible experience—inspiring, challenging, enlightening, and bewildering all at once. All of your senses and faculties come into play, as your fingers learn new tricks, your ears open to new sounds, your brain grapples with new lingo and logic . . . and on top of all this, you've got a complicated six-stringed contraption in your hands that didn't come with any operating instructions. Whether you are at home trying to figure out what to practice or how to change strings, or in a music store shopping for a guitar or a lesson book, reliable and understandable advice can be very hard to find. Myths and misconceptions are everywhere, and the "experts" are often so ensconced in their own little world that their advice blows right over your head or is completely irrelevant to your situation.

That's why this book was created—to be your companion and reference as you learn. From my own experience as a player, to more than a decade of dialogue with guitarists worldwide as the editor of *Acoustic Guitar* magazine and moderator of its on-line forum for beginners, I have heard beginners ask the same types of questions again and again. The 50 most common and perplexing ones are collected and answered here, and all those mystifying bits of guitarese you'll hear are defined along the way (look in the index to find where a particular word or phrase is fully explained and illustrated). Roughly half of the book deals with your instrument itself and its accessories—a source of tremendous confusion for newcomers as well as seasoned players—and the balance is devoted to issues and philosophies of learning. Although the gear discussions do reflect some bias toward acoustic guitars, most of what you will find here is applicable to any beginner playing any type of instrument and studying any style.

Throughout these pages you will hear pearls of wisdom from a wide range of teachers and instrument experts. I can't tell you how many times I have thought, "I wish I had known *that* when I was learning to play!" during the course of doing these interviews and writing this book. I hope the *Beginning Guitarist's Handbook* clears up some nagging questions, steers you away from some dead ends, offers fresh ideas and perspectives, and most of all, energizes you as you travel along this new path.

Good luck, and happy learning.

ALL KINDS OF BEGINNERS

There are many good reasons why the guitar is the most popular instrument in the world today. It's portable, especially the acoustic variety. It can stand alone as a true band-in-a-box, or it can fit into just about any kind of ensemble. It is eminently adaptable, from concert hall to punk club to campfire, and

> **How does the guitar compare to instruments like the piano and violin in terms of learning and the kinds of music you can play?**

it is perhaps the most democratic of instruments. And most important, it is accessible; beginners can learn a few chords and gain access to thousands of songs, and many will continue to play and love the instrument at this level for their whole lives. Yet for those who continue the learning quest, the guitar will unfold infinite levels of nuance and complexity. As master teacher Bill Purse puts it so succinctly, the guitar is "easy to learn, difficult to master."

Some of this holds true for other instruments, but not all of it. The piano is versatile and musically complete, but at least in its grand and upright forms, it isn't an instrument you'll want to lug around town. The violin is nice and portable, but learning to play even a simple melody in tune is a difficult task, and for the most part the music will sound incomplete without supporting instruments.

There are unique aspects to the way a guitar is played that create an intense intimacy between player and instrument. You and your guitar are in extremely close physical contact; you feel it vibrate in your chest and belly, and you cradle it in your arms. Both hands are in contact with the vibrating strings, and unlike on a piano, where you press the keys but a hammer actually sounds the notes, you can create boundless personal variations in the way that you pick, pluck, stroke, tap, and slap a guitar.

In some aspects of learning, other instruments have advantages over the guitar. The linear layout of the piano makes immediate visual sense—low notes to the left, high ones to the right, with a clear pattern of white keys and black keys—and greatly simplifies playing melodies and learning music theory. Once you get past playing basic chords, orienting yourself on the guitar is much trickier: you are constantly moving both horizontally (up and down the neck) and vertically (from one string to the next), and the same pitch can be played at several spots on different strings. The same is true on a violin or mandolin, but those instruments are tuned symmetrically (i.e., each string—or pair of strings on a mandolin—is a fifth above or below the one next to it), while a guitar is not (the strings are tuned in fourths—except for the oddball second string, which is a major third above the third string). The upshot? Generally speaking, guitarists understand their instruments physically/intuitively more than theoretically/intellectually, which has an impact on the kinds of music we make.

As for the appropriateness of particular instruments for particular kinds of music, there are conventions but really no rules. In fact, guitarists seem to get a big kick out of insinuating their instrument into styles of music in which it has never been welcomed in the past. Guitar was an outsider to classical music for many years, but Andrés Segovia broke through the barricades. In traditions from jazz to Celtic music, pioneering players have carried the guitar from the fringe into the spotlight. What's next? It's in your hands, as well as those of guitarists all over the world.

Is there an optimal age for beginning the guitar?

There really isn't—any more than there is a perfect age for all people to get married or have children or take up tennis. We all live and learn according to our own schedules, and the simplest answer is that we are ready to take up the guitar when we are ready to take up the guitar—when we have the desire, the energy, and the time.

Of course, our age and stage of life does significantly affect the learning process. Kids are famously fast learners, with high energy, flexible limbs, and a gift for imitating what they see. But Marcy Marxer, who along with Cathy Fink has been teaching and entertaining both kids and adults for several decades, points out that some things can be harder at a young

age. "The coordination and dexterity it takes to play guitar is often a bigger challenge for kids than it is for adults," she says, "so they need to be patient, as it may take a bit longer. But the one thing kids have is time—they tend to have more free time than adults do.

"Adults have other advantages from having listened longer," she adds. "I once had a student who was in her mid-50s and was playing guitar for the first time. She wanted to learn swing music, so we went in that direction, and all she needed to know was how to play a few chords—she knew automatically how to put them together from how they sounded. She'd say, Oh, that's just like this song or that song. That life experience really helped her."

Carol McComb, a veteran teacher and performer and the author of *Country and Blues Guitar for the Musically Hopeless,* observes that certain aspects of the guitar tend to be easier to learn at certain ages. She says, "For example, fine fingerstyle playing is hard for younger people; I don't think they have developed the motor coordination, by and large, to do it. Some kids are unusual and are OK with it. Teenagers get very coordinated from about 12 on." That coordination remains with adulthood, but she finds that some students over 60, especially those with arthritis, have difficulty getting their fingers to learn basic techniques.

Because of the guitar's close kinship with rock 'n' roll, many of us start to play in our teens, a time in which we (potentially) have not only the coordination but the drive and schedule to devote countless hours to listening, practicing, and poring over guitar magazines—Bill Purse calls hungry young students like these "legends of their own room." Of course that same wellspring of energy can easily be diverted into any number of other activities, leaving the method book or the lessons unfinished.

What it all comes down to, Purse says, is commitment. If we would rather be shopping or flyfishing or surfing the Web than playing the guitar, we won't very likely go far with the instrument. But if we, at whatever age, are truly determined to make music come out of those six strings, we will.

What are some of the signs that a child is ready to learn guitar?

In a way, the signs are the same as they are at any other age—enthusiasm, desire, and the attention span to follow through. But kids, especially those under the age of eight or so, are in a different position from teenagers and older beginners, both because of their still-developing dexterity and because of the very close involvement that their parents will have with any sort of music education.

"If adults set their expectations to a child's developmental stage, any child can play guitar at some level," posits Jessica Baron Turner, whose *SmartStart* guitar method teaches kids from ages five to ten how to strum simple chords in open tunings to accompany familiar songs. "Babies can make sounds," she says. "Toddlers can play a steady beat. Preschoolers can strum a rhythm and sing over an open chord. Kindergartners can learn simple songs and strums, and they can begin to play notes or a one-finger chord. Kids six and up are ready for lessons if they can follow directions, can focus, and are motivated."

Those sentiments are echoed by Los Angeles—based teacher Sonia Michelson, who has developed a method of introducing classical guitar to very young children through a progression of movement games, singing, and ear training along with more formal technical exercises. "I believe a child is ready to learn to play guitar when he or she shows interest and enthusiasm," says Michelson. "However, a very young child (and I do start children as young as three years old with my book *New Dimensions in Classical Guitar for Children*) also needs a supportive parent who will attend each lesson, take notes, and be the home teacher."

Getting an early start on an instrument can be a fantastic thing, as long as the child is having fun and is not being pushed too far and too fast by the parents' desire to give him or her a "head start." A kid who feels forced to sit and practice, who sees playing music as more a parental obligation than a personal pleasure, may actually be worse off in the long run (generations of kids who endured joyless piano lessons can attest to this). By contrast, a child who starts guitar lessons years later but in the meantime soaks up all sorts of music while singing, dancing, and banging sticks on the sidewalk may be more likely to become a lifelong musician. Without the love for it, the learning just won't happen.

The more things change, the more they remain the same. Even with powerful role models like Jewel, Ani DiFranco, and the Dixie Chicks, and an increasing female presence in the music industry, girls who want to play guitar still find themselves confronted with what looks like a boys' club. Often the intimidation factor sets in

I'm a teenage girl interested in playing guitar. I would love to take lessons, but isn't guitar kind of a boy thing?

even before a girl gets her hands on a guitar, right when she comes to the door of your average music store. Margie Mirken from Shade Tree Stringed Instruments in Laguna Niguel, California, who has taught and sold guitars to many teenage girls over the years (and raised a couple of her own), has seen it happen over and over again. She says, "They are used to shopping in woman-friendly situations (soft music; bright, clean, colorful, good-smelling displays; nice, attentive sales-girls), so walking into a bleak rock 'n' roll shop with guys shucking and jiving behind the counter, other customers ronka-ronka-ing on loud electrics, and salesmen ignoring them because they're just little chicks is not the most positive experience. I hear them complain about it all the time."

Not all music stores are like this, and it is amazing how much difference a good, supportive guitar shop can make in the life of any beginner, male or female—not just for buying and repairing your instrument, but often for lessons and workshops and finding new friends with similar musical interests. So scour your local area, ask around, enlist the help of a more experienced friend, and do your homework before you shop (see the Guitar Shopping chapter for tips).

The same thing is true of a sympathetic teacher—he or she can make all the difference. Meet or take trial lessons with several candidates to see who you are most comfortable with. There are many advantages to learning alongside other beginners, so consider taking lessons along with a girlfriend, or look into a (preferably coed) group class, which creates a kind of club to which you automatically belong.

Mirken winds up teaching many of the young girls who come through her shop, and she relates to them through her own experience of learning guitar as a teen. "Most girls tend not to be as aggressive as boys, so I encourage them to dig in a little, to improvise and take chances," she says. "We make a joke of 'not playing like a chick.' They don't have to play like boys, but they should play with the assurance of a musician. And we talk about how to survive in a band situation with guys. I don't care how many fire engines we buy for our daughters, they're still girls. They have to know it's OK to be a girl. They don't have to let the boys push them around or

intimidate them, and they can learn to hold their own in aggressive playing situations."

Along the way, you are bound to run into crusty stereotypes about what girl guitarists do (sing angelically and play simple backup) and don't do (play lead and rock hard). Make sure you don't lose sight of the music that originally lit a fire under you to play guitar, whether it seems like a "boy thing" or not.

You are certainly not alone in asking this question. Many of us look enviously at families where music is like a birthright—where they jam and sing as naturally as breathing and where everyone starts playing an instrument as soon as they can hold one. There *are* some families like this, but the truth is, there are precious few, especially in a cul-

My family isn't musical at all. Will this keep me from getting good at the guitar?

tural environment that favors buying and consuming music over making it yourself. Many lifetime musicians come from parents whose only musical exposure comes in elevators and while they're on hold on the phone.

To clear the way for learning the guitar, the first thing that you need to do is to let go of this idea of "getting good." If we measure success in music by the pleasure we get out of it rather than some external (and probably arbitrary) standard, we can all succeed with an instrument. The guitar is particularly good at offering rewards and satisfaction to players at any level, so there is no reason to think it is beyond your grasp, no matter how rhythmically or melodically challenged you believe you are.

After that, you need to find other people who are in the same boat. Group music classes are great for this, as are the music camps that are found these days all over the country. "One of the great experiences that we've had in the last 20 years," says Cathy Fink, "is teaching at so many of these music camps, where people get into an extremely welcoming atmosphere. They are hanging out with a whole bunch of people just like them—they find out that they're not the only one whose family isn't into music and hasn't been playing all their lives— and there are often organized slow jams for people to play in." These jams, in which teachers lead students in long, slow versions of simple songs, calling out the chords as they go, "create a really nonthreatening atmosphere for making sounds with other people, but nobody is listening particularly to you."

If you have difficulty with the rhythmic aspects of music, Jessica Baron Turner suggests improving your skills through dance and drumming classes and then translating them to the guitar. If you struggle to carry a tune, you could isolate that skill in voice lessons or simply steer away from it; many great players have learned to make the guitar sing because their vocal cords wouldn't do it.

"Nobody is born with a guitar in the hand and the golden voice," Carol McComb reminds us. "Even after people have become fairly accomplished musicians, they still have bad days, and they are still capable of missing even the simplest chord." So don't underestimate yourself—you might be surprised by what you can accomplish even without Mozart's genes or Von Trapp family values.

You could keep your studies private for a while, as you gain confidence, or seek the company of other beginners outside of your family. You could choose a different instrument, which might be good for the family band. Even if one of your sibs got to the guitar before you did, odds are that you will have diverging interests—one of you might be in pursuit of lead-guitar glory, while the other wants to accompany vocals and write songs—so you are essentially playing different instruments. All younger brothers and sisters have this need to make certain interests or activities their own, rather than an imitation of something an older sibling does, but the rivalry is really more a matter of perception than reality. If you feel like you are doing your own thing, you are.

Everyone in my family plays an instrument, and I'm intimidated by how good my siblings are. How can I get over this sense of competition?

Once you get past the initial intimidation, you'll find that all that musical activity in your house is an extraordinary gift. Even the sense of competition can be a blessing in disguise. It certainly was in my family, where my brother started playing guitar first, then lost interest after a year or so—until I got a guitar and started digging into lessons. He couldn't handle the prospect of his younger brother getting ahead, so he picked up his guitar again, and we egged each other on all the way through adolescence, learning much more quickly than either of us would have in isolation. Before long, we were arranging and singing songs together, and then eventually writing, performing, and recording together. And decades later, this shared experience has created a bond that probably wouldn't have developed any other way.

As a grown-up, you may well look enviously at all the kids learning guitar, with seemingly bottomless supplies of time, energy, and confidence in their ability to conquer the six-stringed beast. But you've got some special advantages, too. As noted by Marcy Marxer, your years of listening have given you a lot of intuitive knowledge about the structure and traditions of music, as well as a sense of what specific style(s) you want to play. Your experience in mastering so many new skills, from driving a car to job responsibilities to parenthood,

Any advice for a grown-up beginner with a job and a family?

has undoubtedly given you insight into the ways you learn best—lessons that you can apply to this new quest. And while you may have passed up the chance to be a child prodigy or teen heartthrob, it is never too late to start. Ask any teacher. Cathy Fink tells about a favorite student who picked up guitar at 55. "I went around the room and asked all the beginners what they were doing in the class," she recalls. "This guy said, 'Well, I watched my father when he retired, and he was lonely and bored. That's not going to happen to me, so I got a guitar.'" Too bad that man's father didn't know about the couple in their 90s who once took Carol McComb's beginning class at a music camp!

As an adult beginner, you first need to strategize about time—this project is going to take a regular commitment. Be realistic; it doesn't do you any good to set a goal of practicing three hours a day if there's no hope of actually pulling it off. If you are taking lessons, discuss time issues with your teacher right away. Your playing sessions need not be long: efficient 20-minute practice sessions that tackle specific and achievable goals are more effective than hours of mindless noodling. So set aside small chunks of time at frequent intervals for you and your guitar, and protect them. Finding a space at home where

your kids won't be climbing all over your back while you're playing is not a bad idea either.

There are so many ways to learn guitar these days, from books and videos and CD-ROMs to private and group lessons to music camps, that you can surely find one that matches your schedule and your personality. (Plus, you've got more options than a kid does, considering that you hold the purse strings and presumably have wheels.) Many adults are inclined to study on their own, and there's nothing wrong with that. But many teachers strongly recommend group classes, jams, and music camps as a way to accelerate learning and have big fun in the process. The opportunity to play along with even one other person can bring tremendous rewards. I know several parents who decided to begin playing guitar along with their kids, a special experience for all concerned.

Remember that whenever we are learning something new, we need to allow ourselves to be clumsy and awkward for a while. Kids are more used to this, while grown-ups tend to favor activities that they know well and can do competently and unself-consciously. Jimmy Tomasello, who teaches a wide range of guitar classes at Chicago's Old Town School of Folk Music, notes that "people in adult education are somewhat insecure. And they want to be right—that's a falsehood when you're learning something. The more mistakes you make, the closer you get to reaching the goals that you set for yourself." So cut yourself some slack, take chances, and most of all, enjoy the matchless experience of learning to make music with your own hands.

GUITAR SHOPPING

The guitar family can be sliced and diced and catego-
rized in many ways, and to confuse matters further,
there are numerous instruments that straddle cate-
gories. The most basic distinction is between guitars
that use steel strings and those that use nylon strings.

**What are the different types
of guitars, and what kinds of
music are they used for?**

In North America, **steel-string guitars** are the ones we most often
see and hear. The most common acoustic variety (i.e., guitars that
make music just fine without cords or electrical current) is the **flattop
guitar,** which crops up in countless styles from traditional folk, blues,
and country on down through contemporary unplugged rock.
Typically built with a hollow wooden body and a round soundhole and
patterned after the historic designs of the C.F. Martin and Gibson companies, the flattop guitar is what people usually mean when they say
acoustic guitar. Although any type of guitar can be electrified, the
term **electric guitar** almost always refers to a solid-body steel-string
instrument with one or more magnetic pickups; these guitars (the
archetypal forms being the Fender Stratocaster and the Gibson Les
Paul) are once and forever associated with rock 'n' roll, although they
are used in many other genres as well.

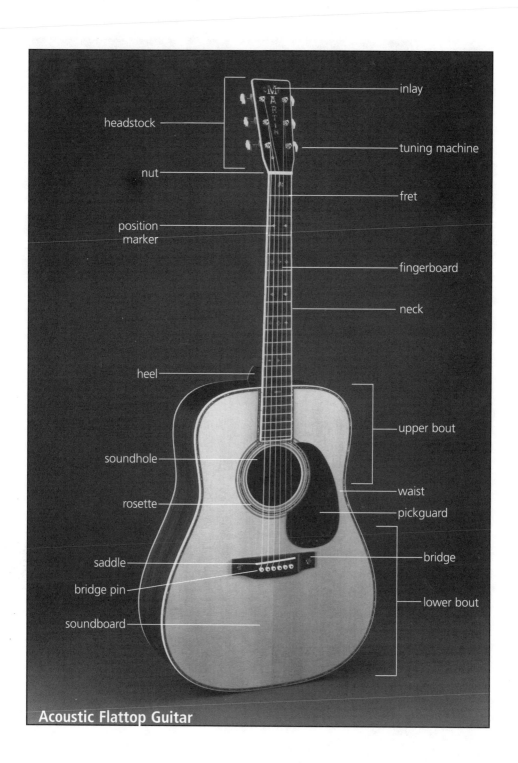

inlay

headstock

tuning machine

nut

fret

position
marker

fingerboard

neck

heel

upper bout

soundhole

waist

rosette

pickguard

saddle

bridge

bridge pin

lower bout

soundboard

Acoustic Flattop Guitar

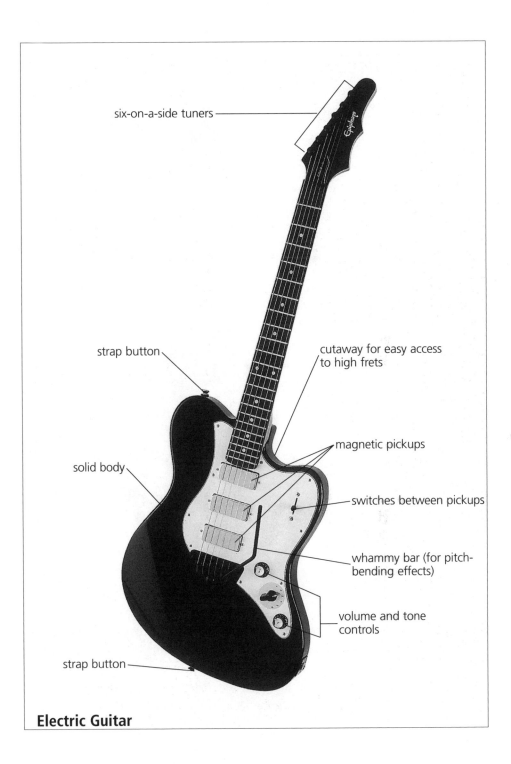

six-on-a-side tuners

strap button

cutaway for easy access to high frets

solid body

magnetic pickups

switches between pickups

whammy bar (for pitch-bending effects)

volume and tone controls

strap button

Electric Guitar

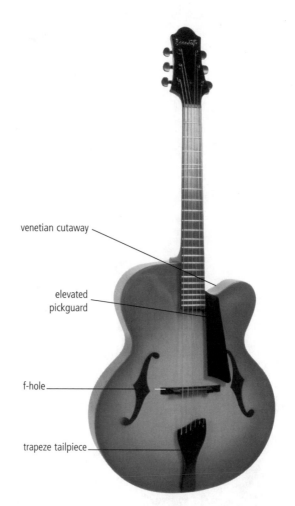

venetian cutaway

elevated
pickguard

f-hole

trapeze tailpiece

Archtop Guitar

Less common types of steel-strings are **archtop guitars,** which take their key design traits from violin-family instruments (*f*-shaped soundholes, arched tops). Archtops began as acoustic instruments, and some are still built that way today, but they are usually played plugged in, producing the mellow, muted sound that we think of as jazz guitar.

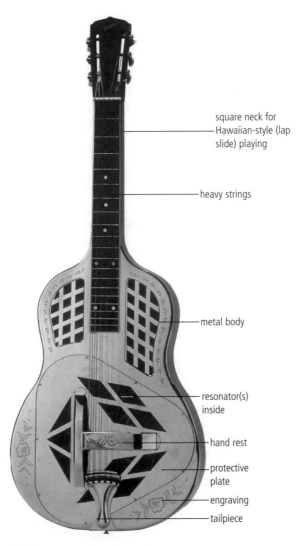

square neck for
Hawaiian-style (lap
slide) playing

heavy strings

metal body

resonator(s)
inside

hand rest

protective
plate

engraving

tailpiece

Resonator Guitar

Further toward the obscure end of the steel-string spectrum are **resonator (or resophonic) guitars.** These guitars have interior aluminum cones that amplify the sound like a loudspeaker does and create a unique sustaining tone. Some resonators are built with metal bodies, others with wood; some are played like regular guitars, while others sit flat across your lap (or are held in a similar position by a

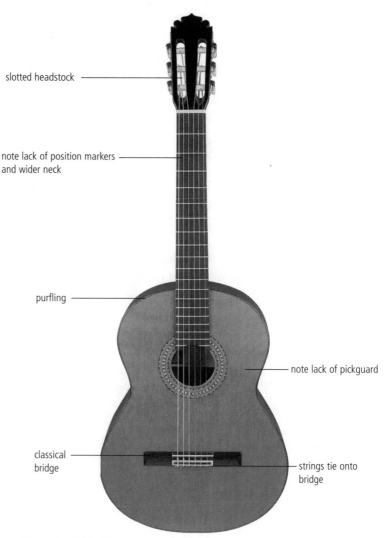

slotted headstock

note lack of position markers and wider neck

purfling

note lack of pickguard

classical bridge

strings tie onto bridge

Classical Guitar

strap) and are played exclusively with a slide—the so-called **Hawaiian style**. These instruments are often referred to by their dominant brand names, **National** and **Dobro,** and have strong associations with blues (especially the metal-body ones) and country/bluegrass (especially the wood-body Dobros played with a slide bar).

While steel-strings rule in North America, **nylon-string guitars** are dominant in most of the rest of the world. Most common is the **classical**

guitar, an acoustic instrument defined by Spanish makers in the 19th and early 20th centuries. Some people call classical guitars **gut-strings,** a reference to the material used for strings before the adoption of nylon in the '50s. As the name suggests, these instruments are traditionally used for classical music and plucked with the fingers (though that never stopped Willie Nelson from battering his old nylon-string with a pick!), and they have wide, flat finger-boards that facilitate classical technique. Nylon-string guitars of this type also are used extensively throughout Latin America for all sorts of indigenous styles.

Flamenco guitars are similar to classicals but are constructed more lightly and from different woods (traditionally cypress for the back and sides rather than rosewood for a classical guitar), and they often have violinlike friction tuning pegs. Flamenco guitars usually have a plastic plate (***golpeador***) to protect the top from the tapping techniques used in flamenco music, and their strings are set up closer to the fingerboard to create an edgier, more percussive tone. These instruments are not often found outside flamenco and the strains of world music they have influenced.

In recent years, amplification technology has inspired new forms of the nylon-string guitar with thin or solid bodies and skinnier necks similar to those found on steel-strings, and these hybrids have

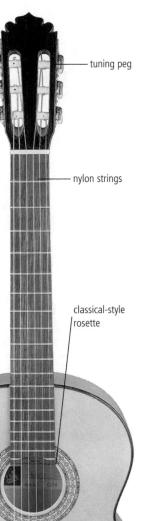

tuning peg

nylon strings

classical-style rosette

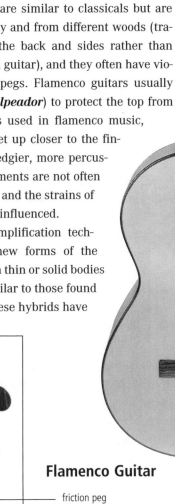

Flamenco Guitar

friction peg

in turn found a home in more and more styles of nonclassical music. The same technological advances have blurred the lines between acoustic and electric guitars—we now have solid-body instruments designed to sound like acoustic instruments when plugged in, and hollow-body instruments that use amplification and effects to sound essentially like electric guitars. Confused? The guitar family tree keeps growing new twigs and branches, presenting players with an amazing array of options.

For more details on the differences between these types of guitars, and what they mean for you as a beginning player, read on.

Is it better to start out with an acoustic or an electric guitar?

Among teachers, there is a pretty strong consensus that it's best to start with an acoustic—that is, unless you are learning guitar because you've always dreamed of cranking up to 11 and doing scissor kicks off the top of your amp, in which case you should definitely ignore this rule of thumb!

So why is the acoustic guitar considered a better beginner instrument? Because it forces you to focus on the fundamentals of technique and sound. It's just you and your guitar, without all the distractions of wires and boxes and amps, which require an entire learning curve of their own. When you play an electric guitar, you are essentially playing the amplifier and the effects pedals as much as you are playing the guitar itself.

Jimmy Tomasello, who teaches guitar and plays in various rock, R&B, and funk bands in the Chicago area, recommends that people start with acoustic guitar even if they ultimately want to play electric. "It is more responsive and more controllable," he says. "One needs to work on dexterity before [addressing] the tone issue of the electric." Since acoustic guitars generally have thicker necks and heavier strings than electrics do, they require more muscle and better technique at the outset. "If you can get a good acoustic tone," he says, "you'll be totally slammin' when you plug in." If, on the other hand, you start on an electric and then pick up the acoustic later on, you will likely have a much harder time building the necessary strength and chops.

And then there are the diplomatic benefits of going unplugged. "No one wants to hear a beginner blasting out," Tomasello adds. "It will aid your relationship with family or roommates!"

Is learning the acoustic steel-string completely different from learning classical guitar?

In many respects, yes. The differences start with the instruments themselves. The string materials sound and feel radically different: Steel strings are sharper, louder, and more aggressive sounding, while nylon creates a softer, more melodious tone. Thin steel strings dig painful grooves into the fingertips of beginners, while nylon strings are fatter and gentler, which is why classical guitars are typically recommended for kids and sometimes for older beginners. Standard classical guitars have wider necks than steel-strings do, which makes for tougher left-hand stretches but in the long run makes possible the kinds of intricate fingerwork that define classical guitar music. Traditionally, classical guitars are played with the guitar resting against a left leg elevated by a footstool, again to facilitate the kind of movement around the neck required in classical music; by contrast, steel-string players hold their guitars sitting and standing in all sorts of idiosyncratic positions— —virtually every way *except* the classical position with a footstool. Classical players carefully maintain long right-hand fingernails for plucking the strings; some steel-string players do this too, but many more simply use a pick or their bare fingers and never worry about their nails.

The traditional classical playing position, with footstool.

The differences go deeper, down into the way the instruments are taught. Classical guitar teachers emphasize reading music, learning composed pieces, and mastering strictly controlled techniques, while teachers of the steel-string, with its roots in folk and rock, are much more apt to focus on playing songs by ear. The former lays a foundation for a long road of learning, while the latter offers more instant gratification. There are many points on which a classical- and a folk- or rock-oriented teacher will disagree, right down to the "correct" position of your hands. They even use different languages; you will hear terms like **rest stroke** and **free stroke** (two basic ways to strike a string with your finger), for example, only from a classical teacher. These are all sweeping generalizations, of course, but the fact is that nylon- and steel-string guitars offer very different sounds, and they are separated by a cultural, pedagogical, and technical divide.

Guitarists making the switch from one instrument and approach to the other need to make many adjustments. Those steeped in classical studies will probably find their strong technical foundation to be an advantage on the steel-string, even if they wind up not using some techniques specific to the classical style. But they also may have trouble starting to improvise and play by ear, just as steel-string players switching to classical may struggle with written notation and learning by rote. Ben Harbert, a classical player and the head of guitar teaching at the Old Town School of Folk Music, points out that "much of classical guitar uses open chords or pieces of open chords. Classical students who have some experience with steel-string styles can take a lot of the left hand over to classical. Also, the steel-string student achieves success early on, granting an element of confidence when beginning classical. On the other hand, guitarists are often intimidated by classical studies. Many of my classical students become burdened by correcting bad habits that they developed learning another style: the left-hand thumb position (thumb poking up and above the guitar neck), the right hand plucking across the strings rather than pushing the strings down into the body of the guitar . . . I could go on."

If you haven't played either instrument and are trying to make a choice, you should follow your gut response to the sound and repertoire of the guitars themselves. "Students should learn the music that interests them," says Harbert. "Most people follow paths from genre to genre. Often a student will become interested in another style that warrants a new instrument: for instance, going from Black Sabbath to Randy Rhoads to classical guitar, as many guitarists did in the '80s."

Finally, keep in mind that the classical approach is only one way to learn the nylon-string. It is entirely possible to play jazz or folk or new age or whatever style on a nylon-string, just as it is entirely possible (though less common) to take a more formal, classical approach to the steel-string. So if you are attracted to the sound of one instrument but the repertoire of another, you can choose a less-traveled path.

What should I consider in choosing between a straight acoustic and an acoustic-electric?

In recent years, amplification systems for acoustic guitars have gone from being an option to being practically standard equipment. In many cases, manufacturers have simply added pickups to their existing acoustic models, and the acoustic properties of the instruments are not affected by the retrofitting. But an increasing

on-board controls

smaller, shallower body

under-saddle piezo pickup

Acoustic-Electric Guitar

number of instruments are designed from the ground up with amplification in mind, and they strike a compromise between acoustic and electric sound: they tend to be thinner bodied and have less unplugged volume and presence, but they can sound great plugged in and be more trouble-free on stage.

So your choice really hinges on whether the acoustic or amplified sound is more important to you. What do you see yourself doing with this instrument, now and down the road? Margie Mirken of Shade Tree Stringed Instruments says that from her perspective "the most important things are tone and playability, so a pickup system takes a backseat. But I remember as a kid being fascinated with trying out new picks and learning to use a strap and stand up. After teaching for many years, I understand that the little accoutrements can add to the flavor of the learning experience. If a student thinks it's fun to plug in and make a big sound even before he or she is ready to get a gig, so much the better. Have a blast. But I also see people who've bought a really bad guitar (bad tone, back neck angle, bad frets, horrible playability) with a pickup system, and it's apparent that the manufacturer put all the money into the electronics. The student is really loud but sounds terrible."

In the end, you are buying a guitar first and a pickup system second, and you need to make sure the guitar is a good one that you can grow with. Keep in mind that pickup systems can be very easily and inexpensively added to acoustic instruments, so if you are not sure you want or need to plug in, you should get the best straight acoustic you can and see how your interests develop over time. Also remember that amplification technology is changing constantly, so this year's standard will become quickly obsolete. Acoustic-electric guitars with built-in pickup systems, especially those with control panels cut into the side of the instruments, commit you to the current technology, so you may be better off with a system that can be added, removed, and upgraded as your needs change.

As noted earlier, nylon-string classical guitars are widely recommended for young kids, mostly because they are much softer on the fingertips than steel strings. "With kids, the nylon strings make the guitar a little more accessible," says Cathy Fink. "Making it easier on their fingers is going to make it more fun for them, and most of them are not even at a place where they have a goal of, I want to play this kind of music, and I want to play that kind of guitar. With adults, if they know they want a steel-string instrument, then they may as well start on a steel-string instrument instead of starting on nylon and changing."

Should a child start with nylon or steel strings? How can you tell if a guitar is the right size?

After the age of seven or eight, a child may be able to handle steel strings—especially on a well-made guitar, with light-gauge strings, that has been professionally adjusted for playability. In general, today's entry-level steel-strings are much easier to play than the typical budget model from a few decades ago, which had, as Emmylou Harris once described her first guitar, "a neck like a baseball bat and strings that were about six inches off the neck."

No matter what type of strings you choose, finding the right size guitar is critical. Some kids manage to learn by heroically reaching over a full-size guitar, but young ones will be much more comfortable with a half- or three-quarter-size or otherwise downscaled model. There are a number of good-quality instruments available in these fractional sizes; these little guitars often double as travel instruments for grown-ups.

Sonia Michelson, who teaches classical guitar to children as young as three, says, "It

Several companies offer classical guitars in fractional sizes, like these Amadas.

is very important that the child can easily put his arm on the upper bout of the guitar and at the same time find it comfortable to reach and play the strings near the soundhole. It goes without saying that it should be easy to tune the guitar and that the sound produced is a good one."

Marcy Marxer offers another size guideline that worked well in her very musical family. "When I was a kid, the rule was you had to be as tall as the guitar before you were allowed to get one. I think part of the reason is that when the guitar sits on your lap, if you're not that long and you haven't grown quite that much, you're not going to be able to comfortably reach the fingerboard. You're going to be stretching too much."

The top guitar is too much of a stretch for both arms, while the bottom one (equipped with a capo to further shorten the neck) is a good fit.

To find the right fit, have your child hold guitars of various sizes and see if she can put her hands into playing position without straining. Her left arm should bend comfortably when she reaches all the way down to the first fret; if the arm is fully extended and straight, the neck is too long. One good temporary solution to this problem is attaching a capo, which shortens the neck and can be moved or removed as the child grows (see the capo question in Equipment Basics).

As you shop for kids' guitars, you are likely to encounter guitars for prices that seem too good to believe, especially in toy stores and other outlets that don't ordinarily carry musical instruments. Resist the temptation to buy one of these ultra-cheapos if you want your kid to actually learn to play rather than treat the guitar as another toy that will be gathering dust in the bottom of the closet within a few weeks or months. "I'm sure there's a correlation between kids who wash out of playing and the quality of their instruments," says Margie Mirken. "There's a difference between functional but not exciting and a piece of junk that will not tune or play." A modest investment of another $50 or $100 for a real instrument might make all the difference for your young player.

Yes, you might need to buy a left-handed guitar, and yes, you might do fine playing a regular righty model. Remember, playing the guitar isn't like handwriting or throwing a baseball; you need *both* hands to make music on the thing. As Bill Purse points out to people who ask this question, there is no such thing as a left-handed piano.

I am left-handed. Do I need to buy a special lefty guitar, or should I learn to play a regular model?

So try a regular right-handed model for awhile, and see how it feels. Your two hands are being asked to do very different tasks: the right hand carries the rhythm and drives the sound by strumming or picking, mostly using large motor coordination of the arm, while the left makes smaller, more precise finger movements between strings and frets. In a way, says Jessica Baron Turner, this is a logical division of labor for a lefty, because the dominant hand is assigned the more sophisticated task, which also requires more strength, at least in the fingers.

But that doesn't change the fact that for some southpaws, playing this way will just feel *weird*. You may really want to strum those strings with your left hand, no matter how many times you try it the other way. If this is true for you, by all means make the switch. Unfortunately, you can't simply flip the guitar over to play lefty, because the strings are then in the opposite order: the ones with the lowest pitch (the bass strings) are now down closest to the floor, while the highest strings are up toward the ceiling. Although a few guitarists have bucked tradition and made great music this way (notably Elizabeth Cotten, who wrote the folk classic "Freight Train"), a flopped-over guitar literally turns conventional technique upside down: you play treble notes with your thumb and bass notes with your fingers, rather than the other way around. If you play upside down, good luck—you won't find much help from any teacher or book!

Notice how the string order and angle of the saddle are reversed on these righty and lefty models.

When shopping for a lefty guitar, you may find a few options in your local music store, but don't feel limited by what's on the rack, because just about any model can be special-ordered as a lefty. It is also fairly easy and inexpensive for a repairer to convert a righty guitar to a lefty by changing the nut and (on a steel-string guitar) the saddle to accommodate the reverse string order.

Is it a good idea to borrow or rent a guitar instead of buying a new one right away?

If you are not sure whether your relationship with the guitar is going to be a brief fling or a long-term commitment, borrowing or renting an instrument can be a smart way to go. It's also a great way to test-drive your options if you don't know what type or size of instrument you want—steel- or nylon-string, flattop or Telecaster—or even if you already have an instrument but wonder if a different one might be better. Music stores that offer guitar classes often have good deals for students to rent their stock instruments, and they are likely to supply you with a guitar that is set up properly and easy to play. Trying out instruments like this will make you a much more savvy shopper when you're ready to buy one of your own.

If a friend offers you a loaner or you discover an old guitar that's been sitting in Uncle Bob's attic for years, make sure the instrument is a good fit for you and in decent playing condition (topics taken up later in this chapter) before you count yourself lucky. Get thee to a guitar shop with a reputable repair department: a setup and a new set of strings may cost you $35 or $50, but it might make the difference between actually learning and giving up after doing battle with a beast that is unplayable by even the most iron-handed pro. A trip to the shop also might inform you that the instrument has some fatal flaw, such as a warped neck or a sunken top, that will doom both your efforts to get a decent sound and the repairer's efforts to make the thing playable at a reasonable cost.

Renting or borrowing also makes sense if your budget would only allow you to get into the very lowest end of the new guitar market. Beg or borrow (don't steal) a guitar for a while as you save a few more bills for an instrument with real staying power, as explained further in the next question.

What's the difference between a $200 and a $2,000 acoustic guitar?

Trying to discern the differences between guitars separated by hundreds or even thousands of dollars on their price tags can be tricky, especially for a newcomer to the instrument. Modern factories are very skilled with cosmetic details, so that even very inexpensive guitars can look downright fancy. Complicating matters further is the fact that as you move up the price scale, the objective differences in quality from one guitar to the next diminish, and the judgment about which one is better becomes much more a matter of personal preference.

In the extremely competitive field of guitar retailing, prices are always in flux and eminently negotiable, but we can draw some rough guidelines about what you'll find in different ranges. The prices cited below are list prices; the actual amount you pay at the store will be approximately 10 to 35 percent less, depending on the manufacturer's discounting policies and the retailer's eagerness to put the guitar into your hands.

UNDER $500

Guitars in this budget category are produced in large batches in factories, and their across-the-board quality has notched up in recent years—great news for beginners. Also great news is the fact that steel-string guitars in this price range are now available in a few body sizes, whereas in the past almost all were large, dreadnought-sized instruments, which can be tough going for smallish players.

One of the defining features of guitars in this budget category is the use of **laminated woods** (multiple, very thin sheets of wood glued together) rather than **solid woods** like those found on higher-end instruments. Laminates are stable and easy to work with in the

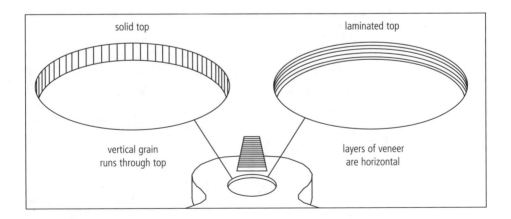

factory, and guitars made with them can sound good. But all-laminate guitars don't have the physical strength or tonal character of solid-wood guitars, which are renowned for the way the sound opens up over time as the instrument gets "played in." Above $300 list or so, you will find guitars with solid tops (usually spruce) and laminate backs and sides (rosewood, mahogany, and other woods), which are a significant step up in quality from all-laminate guitars— not just because of the top, but because these instruments usually get better materials overall and more attention to detail. (They also might come with essentials like cases and warranties, which the $200 model may not include.) You can learn to spot a solid top by looking at the edge of the soundhole: if it's solid, you'll see the grain lines running all the way through the top; if it's laminated, the grain lines will be broken (on some guitars, though, those lines can be tricky to see).

If you can swing it with your budget, by all means go for a solid-topped model, which is more likely to continue satisfying you tonally over the years and is built to last. Scoring a solid top in this price range usually means skipping some frills and cosmetic touches, like decorative inlays and a high-gloss finish, a trade-off that is well worth making. Ditto for budget models with pickups: you're better off with a straight acoustic model if the manufacturer has skimped on the fundamentals in order to include the electronics.

One of the most persistent myths about factory guitars is that they are identical down to the last detail. It ain't so—hands and machines collaborate on building all guitars, and each piece of wood is different, so a rack of instruments of the same model from the same factory will vary in construction quality, tone, and playability. This is especially true in this price range, where the quality control is not as strict as in more expensive guitars. So look and listen closely, and engage the help of someone with experience to determine if the particular guitar you are interested in is well constructed and can be adjusted, now and tomorrow, for smooth and easy playing.

$500 TO $1,000

Just a few years ago, this was a fairly unpromising price range, mostly filled with gussied-up versions of imported budget instruments. But along came a computer revolution in guitar manufacturing, which has allowed factories everywhere to turn out basic versions of their much more expensive models for unprecedented low prices. In the late 1990s, North American companies broke the $1,000 price barrier for all-solid-wood guitars, a sonic boom that echoes across the guitar market today.

When you reach this price range, you should expect the guitars to be well made, with clean construction and a higher grade of materials, and protected by hard-shell cases and limited lifetime warranties. Like solid-topped guitars under $500, all-solid-wood guitars under $1,000 are likely to be relatively plain compared to their more expensive brethren. But instruments like these represent an incredible opportunity for players to own guitars fundamentally like those that used to be available only for $1,500 and much more. If you start out with a budget instrument but later want to upgrade, it makes a lot of sense to aim for this all-solid-wood threshold.

In the under-$1,000 range you'll also find good-quality guitars made from a combination of laminated and solid woods, as well as acoustic-electric instruments (some full-size, some thin-body) with sophisticated pickup systems that make great stage guitars. Usually these guitars feature easy-access tone and volume controls on the upper bout of the guitar, which can be very handy but, as noted in the above discussion of acoustic-electrics, mean that your guitar has a large hole cut in the side that will be there forever. So if you are getting an on-board amplification system like this, make sure you want it.

$1,000 TO $2,500

Once you are up into four figures, you can pick from a wide range of professional-quality guitars built in factories with all solid woods. List prices for top models by famous names like Martin and Gibson will run higher—sometimes way higher—than $2,500, but these companies offer plenty of options in this range. Stan Jay of the venerable music store Mandolin Brothers in Staten Island, New York, says that the quality of these instruments is reflected in all stages of their manufacture. "All processes are performed at a high level, from the layering of lacquer, continuously buffed out, resprayed, and buffed again, to the selection of wood **purflings** [the strips of wood around the edge of the body], to the shadings and the stainings, to the installation of precision componentry. It should certainly approach flawless work. The sound should be lush, the sustain palpable."

The difference between the $1,200 model and the $2,400 model becomes a matter of materials and appointments—the cheaper one might have a lower grade or different type of wood, satin rather than gloss finish, plain dot fingerboard markers rather than elaborate inlays. Upper-end amplification systems also add substantially to your cost. As with any consumer product, intangible factors like brand reputation and perceived value definitely affect how guitars are priced. Sometimes there is less difference from one to the next than meets the eye or the ear of even an experienced player. If the cheaper one delivers for you, tonally and aesthetically, go for it.

OVER $2,500

You'll still find large-factory guitars at prices from here on up to the stratosphere for limited editions and such. But you'll also find a greatly expanded universe of options, which includes instruments from small- and medium-sized shops (e.g., Collings, Santa Cruz, and Lowden) and the army of individual **luthiers** out there designing and building guitars on their own.

"A $3,000 acoustic guitar," says Stan Jay, "would be favorably compared to the guitars of the major makers that were made during their '**vintage**' period, a time when procedures were followed or woods were chosen that are no longer routinely available in those factories. The golden era for the acoustic guitar was 1929 to 1946. For electrics, it was 1949 to 1969. A $3,000 new guitar comes very close to re-creating the quality of performance and tone that one might have obtained from a guitar made during its golden era at the time of its original sale."

At this level, practically anything can be customized—for a price, of course. In contrast to the factory assembly line, instruments in this range are built with quite a lot of attention to the characteristics of specific pieces of wood and how they work together in a particular guitar—trained hands make subtle adjustments to get the most out of each guitar. Especially with individual makers, attention is also paid to your particular needs and desires as a player, not just for custom visual details but for your playing style, preferred strings, and planned uses for the instrument (home, stage, studio).

So back to the $1,800 question: Is a $2,000 guitar *that* much better than a $200 guitar? Well, yes. The pricey instrument is definitely more refined and probably quite a bit easier to play; its sound has more depth and nuance and will improve over time, and if cared for properly, it will last for at least a lifetime. The budget guitar sounds as good now as it will ever sound, and it won't survive nearly as long as the boutique model. But if the $200 or $300 guitar gets you on your way as a player, that's the most important job an instrument can ever do. And when you are ready to move into an instrument with more potential—and you will know when that moment has arrived—many great guitars await you.

There are a few size factors that you should be aware of as a guitar shopper. First and most obvious, there is the body size—a primary consideration for acoustic instruments. In steel-string guitars, beyond down-

What sizes of guitars are available, and how can I tell if an instrument fits me well?

scaled instruments for kids and travelers and the occasional "baby" models (some of which are tuned higher than standard tuning), you'll find an array of standard sizes including, from smallest on up: **parlor**, **concert** or **0** (pronounced "oh"), **grand concert** or **00** ("double oh"), **auditorium** or **OM/000** ("triple oh"), **grand auditorium**, **dreadnought**, and **jumbo.** Toward the smaller end of the spectrum falls the standard classical guitar body. The way these and other terms get tossed around in the guitar world may make your head spin (just try figuring out what is meant by "small jumbo," for instance!), but what is more important than a model's history or anatomy is the way it feels and sounds in your arms.

The powerful, hefty dreadnought has been the standard flattop guitar for many decades, but this is not a situation of one size fits all. "If you get a small man or small woman or a younger person and hand

Standard Acoustic Body Sizes

3/4 size 5   Concert 0   Concert Standard 0   Grand Concert   Grand Concert 00
(12 fret)   Standard

them a dreadnought," says Carol McComb, "it can be impossible for them to actually play it. It's too big to reach around and play without having to hold it in some really odd, awkward manner. Most women who are small look dwarfed by a large guitar."

Pay attention to how your right arm and shoulder feel as you reach over the guitar and down to the strings, a function of both the dimensions of the top and the depth of the sides. Comfort is essential; contorting your body will not only make it harder to play, it may injure you in the long run. "The more experienced player will instinctively know, by trying many examples, what size feels right," says Stan Jay. "A novice may not immediately know, but trial without time pressure is recommended." Ergonomic considerations aside, different body sizes offer different sonic possibilities, and you may find yourself over time gravitating from one to another, or acquiring a couple of instruments of varied sizes. In my own case, over a couple of decades I've gone from dreadnought to bassy jumbo to trebly grand concert to something right in the middle as my ear and playing ability have developed.

The other important size considerations relate more to your fretting hand. The neck shape (or **neck profile**) will vary considerably from model to model—if you cut a bunch of necks in cross-section,

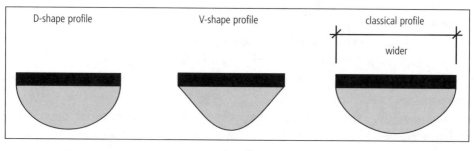

Neck Profiles

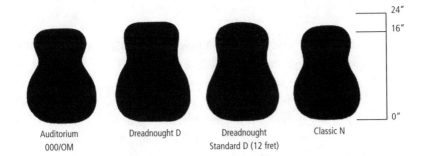

Auditorium 000/OM   Dreadnought D   Dreadnought Standard D (12 fret)   Classic N

some would look rounded (like a D), others more pointed (like a V); electric guitars and acoustics adopting their characteristics have much thinner necks than traditional acoustics do. The **scale length,** or vibrating length of the string, affects your reach from fret to fret as well as the tension you feel on the strings (a longer scale length will generally feel harder to play). The **fingerboard width** is an important factor too, because it affects how far apart the strings are, which in turn affects what you do with both hands. Classical guitars have wider fingerboards (typically two inches wide) than steel-strings, which are often in the range of 1¾ to 1¹¹⁄₁₆ inches. Does that tiny fractional difference in width really matter? It does, although as Margie Mirken points out, "Whatever you start on will feel normal." People with big hands don't necessarily need guitars with fat fingerboards, but if you chronically feel as if your fingers are battling for space down on the fretboard, you might try out a model with wider string spacing for a while and see if it makes a difference. It's worth noting that fingerstyle (as opposed to pick) players tend to prefer wider necks, so your technique can be a factor too.

In any case, the key to finding your way through all these options is pretty simple, not to mention pretty entertaining: play lots and lots of guitars. In these boom times for the guitar, options abound. A shop with a diverse selection and a nonpressured atmosphere will greatly streamline the process of finding the right fit.

One of the toughest things in guitar shopping, especially for a beginner, is recognizing what are fatal flaws in an instrument—problems that are either unrepairable or too expensive to repair given the value of

> **What are the most important structural flaws to look for when checking out a new guitar? How about used?**

the guitar—and what aspects of how it feels and plays are easily adjustable in the course of a routine setup.

Let's take the latter category first. Setup work, which will be described in more detail in the next chapter, addresses several aspects of the guitar's sound and feel, but of particular significance to you is the ***action***: the height of the strings off the fingerboard. High action makes it more difficult to press the strings down to the fingerboard, so you generally want the action to be as low as possible without causing the strings to buzz. The other major factor is the strings themselves—lighter-gauge strings will ease the work of your fingers. So if you love everything else about a guitar (the look, the tone, the price) but find it harder to play than others, see if some simple tweaks or a lighter set of strings might make the difference. The same goes for a guitar with a buzz problem: it might be easily fixable. Old, dirty strings will keep a guitar from staying in tune and remove all of the sparkle from the sound, too; don't hesitate to ask for a new set if the guitar you're checking out sounds really dead. The need for small adjustments like these should not deter you from buying a guitar—they are standard procedure and should be part of your purchase.

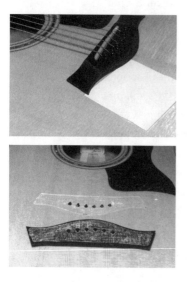

If you can slide a piece of paper under the bridge, it will need to be removed and reglued.

Then there are the flaws that should make you put that guitar right back on the rack. "In the fatal category," says Stan Jay, "incorrect **neck angle** (usually when the action's too high and there's no way to lower it) is the most common and least remediable flaw." Other less-common problems on his list include: a wavy fingerboard, uneven frets, insufficient play in the truss rod, unstable top (look out for bulges or depressions), off-center strings, and bad **intonation** (i.e., notes up the neck that sound out of tune).

One way to check the intonation is to learn to play a harmonic at the 12th fret: while lightly touching (not pressing down) a string with your left hand exactly over the 12th fret, pick the same string with your right hand. When you hit it just right, you should hear a chiming tone that continues even when you take your finger away from the string. On each string, compare the 12th-fret harmonic to the note you get when you press down the string at the same fret. If these two notes do not sound in tune with each other, the guitar has an intonation problem.

Your best insurance against these flaws is simple: choose a good shop in the first place. "A well-run guitar shop will not wait for the customer to discover such guitars," says Jay. "Each incoming guitar should follow a specified check-in procedure, and any that do not meet the 'implied warranty of merchant-ability' rule should be pulled out and returned to the manufacturer. They should never see the showroom floor."

As for used guitars, all the above rules of thumb still apply. But an instrument that has been used (or abused) for some years might have picked up some other problems too—especially nicks and scratches and cracks. Some of these are purely cosmetic and some are structural, and if you discover anything like this on an instrument you're considering, you should definitely enlist the help of an experienced eye that can tell the difference.

For researching a guitar purchase, the Web is a useful tool; just about every manufacturer has extensive photos and specifications available at the click of a mouse. But as a shopping medium, it leaves a lot to be desired. You might be able to look at a picture of the instrument, but that's not the same as seeing it in person and holding it and hearing it. Maybe you can download a sound sample, but that won't tell you much of anything, because the sample is more a product of the player and the recording technique than an objective measure of the instrument itself—and it certainly won't tell you what the guitar will sound and feel like strummed by your own fingers. Even if you have done hands-on investigation and decided on a maker and a model, buying it on-line is a risky proposition, because there will be differences—sometimes significant ones—from one example to the next. Getting a good setup is an essential part of buying a guitar, too, and the on-line retailer leaves you to commission this work separately from a repairer who doesn't have a vested interest in keeping you happy with that instrument.

> **Where's the best place to shop for a guitar—the local shop, the music superstore, pawnshops, the Internet?**

So until the day comes when you can download a demo guitar from the Web, you should buy your instrument in the real-time, physical world. Your options in retail stores will vary considerably depending on where you live, but let's take a look at what an ideal shop would be like, whether it's a mom-and-pop outfit or a chain superstore. It would have a wide but carefully selected array of instruments, reasonable prices, knowledgeable salespeople who don't start counting their commission when you walk in the door but who give you the time and space to think clearly, quiet rooms where you can play instruments as long as you like, a respectful attitude toward women shoppers and beginners of all ages, an active repair shop with a reputation for good warranty and nonwarranty service, and a teaching studio in case you want lessons. Sound utopian? A far cry from the Guitar Qwikee Mart in your town? Well, we all do the best we can with what we've got.

The point is, though, that the place you buy your guitar is very important. In fact, going to a good shop substantially increases the odds that you'll wind up with an instrument that is right for you. Even if you know exactly what you want and can save a few bucks bargaining with the sharks across town, you may wind up spending the difference and more on "extras" like setup work and a new set of strings—things that the other shop would throw in for free. A relationship with a good music store will be valuable to you as long as you play the guitar—long after the "deal" you cut with the sharks is forgotten.

That's not to say that good deals cannot be gotten from music stores, whether they be schooled with sharks or minnows. But when you are shopping in an environment where the salespeople are clueless or untrustworthy (or when you're on the Web and essentially on your own), you've really got to know what you want, what you're looking at, and what it's worth. You've got to be able to spot the guitar with a neck that is at such a low angle that it will soon develop a permanent, unfixable buzz (as mentioned above, a good shop will actually put a lemon like this right back into a box marked "Return to Sender"). You've got to have a clear enough sense of your own preferences that you won't be talked into a different model that just happens to bring the sales guy a higher commission. In other words, a good music store allows you to relax and make your decision in an unhurried, unstressful, and confident fashion.

So you are ready to buy a guitar—you have done some thinking and research about the basic types of instruments and narrowed the field; you have found a music store or two that carries the kinds of guitars you're interested in; and you've got some money saved and have set a preliminary budget for yourself (including some allowance for lessons and instructional materials). Here are some tips on how to complete the process.

What's the best way for a beginner to shop for a guitar? Should I get help from a teacher or a friend?

Be patient. "Give yourself time to try out a lot of guitars," says Mark Dvorak, a guitarist, banjoist, and teacher at the Old Town School of Folk Music. "I think it's important to feel that the decision to buy has not been rushed. Hands-on experience and good information make for an informed decision. If you are already enrolled in lessons or a class, you might feel an urgency to pick out an instrument right away. Borrowing a playable instrument is a cheap solution. And renting a playable instrument is money well spent, in my opinion, even if you wind up renting for an extended period of time.

"If the guitar is to become a part of your life, you and your instrument are going to be spending a lot of time together. Students who spend a month or two or six trying out a dozen or more guitars and listening to what people have to say about different models will put themselves in a good position to select an instrument they will be happy with over the long haul."

Along the way, watch out for salespeople at the car dealership— oops, I mean music store—who hit you with any variation of the opening line, "Are you planning on going home with a guitar today?" Needless to say, their commissions and sales targets, and not your long-term satisfaction, are foremost in their minds. Don't let them push you into a hasty decision (in fact, I highly recommend turning right around and taking your business elsewhere).

Get recommendations. You will find that advice is very easy to come by. Guitar magazines and music Web sites offer a steady stream of information, reviews, and new product announcements. Friends and acquaintances will be happy to offer their opinions, and Web forums are packed with people who are just dying to tell you exactly which guitar to buy. On-line discussions can be useful because they pull together people of similar interests from all over the place, but then again, you don't have any idea who the individuals behind the screen handles are, and they don't have any idea who you are. Beware of those who seem intent on trashing one brand and putting another on a pedestal. Think of yourself as a political pollster, and pay more attention to general trends in what people recommend than in a single person's (especially a stranger's) opinion.

And don't make your decision solely on these third-party recommendations. Instead, use them to help you draft a list of guitars to try for yourself and to give you a general idea about what they might cost.

Bring along a helper. The key to making the right decision is confidence, and if having a friend along increases your comfort level, definitely bring one. Many guitar teachers will help students choose an instrument (it is worth at least knowing that in some cases, teachers receive a commission from a music store for their referral—but if your teacher is straightforward and trustworthy, this arrangement shouldn't cause any particular conflict of interest).

Margie Mirken recommends that beginners bring a helper along, but she cautions that "many fairly experienced players don't know anything about guitars, either, so don't let them make the decision for you. Avoid someone who has an ego to feed with your guitar budget." Also don't bother bringing along someone who plays in a completely different style from what you are interested in (e.g., a classical player wouldn't be much help in trying out electric guitars) or who steers you toward these cool $1,500 guitars rather than the $400 models you actually are considering.

Practice a few try-out songs. If you can play at least a little, practice a few songs, chord progressions, or picking patterns so that you can play them smoothly and unself-consciously in front of others. In addition to playing chords, advises renowned guitar teacher and author Frederick Noad, "it is worth learning in advance how to play single notes, so as to be able to try the high reaches as well as the low positions." Not only will a little rehearsal put you more at ease in the store, but it will mean that you are comparing apples to apples—you'll be playing the same pieces on a series of guitars and hearing how each one responds. If you strum one guitar with a pick, fingerpick the next one, then play a little lead on the next one, you will have very misleading ideas about how they compare.

Hearing someone else (your helper or one of the salespeople) demo the guitars can be instructive too, especially if you are just starting to play.

Look as well as listen. Obviously you want a guitar that sounds good, with all the structural features discussed above. But looks matter too, even though you may run across players who insist they don't. The ideal guitar for you, as bluesman Steve James once put it, "makes ou feel like playing every time you so much as look at it."

Watch for hidden costs. Be savvy about prices and get the best deal can, but consider the factors that lie behind the price tag. Is a included? A new set of strings, picks, a capo? What are the return policies? What kind of warranty or repair support will Some inexpensive guitars come with manufacturers' warothers do not, but often what matters to you more than the from a distant corporation is the service you get from ou actually bought your guitar.

ppers today is that there are many well-made, nstruments available with a lot of music in r a needle in a haystack—you're looking s that will be very satisfying for you to your homework, taken your time, and uitar you can afford, take it home.

y

you
setup
store's
you get?
ranties and o
piece of paper
the place where

The good news
attractive, ine
them. You ar
for one of a
own and
feel a s
Congra

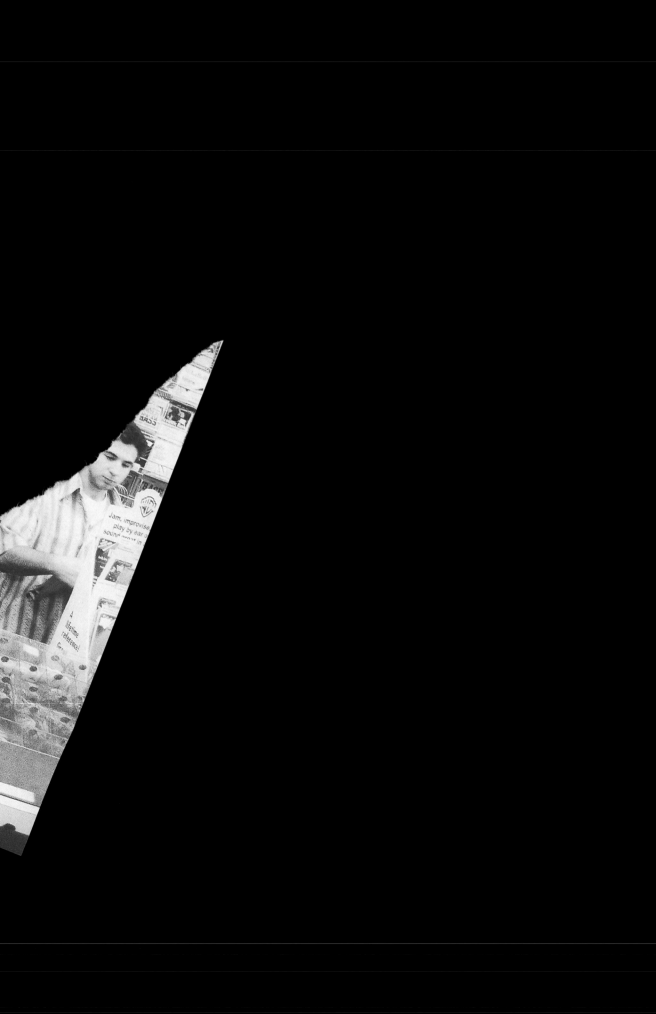

EQUIPMENT BASICS

A **setup** is a series of adjustments to your guitar that keep it playing and sounding its best. Guitars are not static objects—over time the forces of climate, string tension, and playing make small but significant changes in factors such as the **action** (the height of the strings from the fingerboard), which, in turn, dramatically affect how your guitar sounds and feels. A setup might fix something as obvious as a loudly buzzing string or do something as subtle as making barre chords a little easier to play.

What is a guitar setup, and why is it so important?

So a guitar setup, best done at a professional repair shop, is not unlike the 30,000-mile checkup for your car. The difference is that a new guitar probably needs a setup even before you take it home for the first time. A sign of sloppy work in the factory? Not necessarily. Guitars are given a general setup before being shipped from the manufacturer, and a shop may tweak them further before hanging them on the rack. But a good setup involves optimizing a specific guitar for a specific player, and that can be done for you only with your input.

The things most commonly adjusted during a setup are the nut, the saddle, and the truss rod. Let's take a look at what these are and how they might be attended to during a setup.

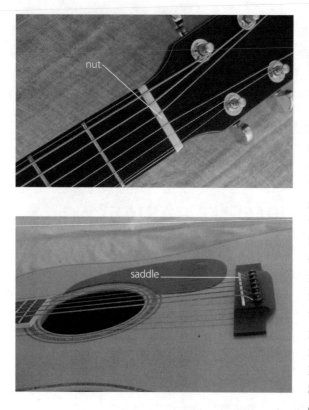

The **nut** is the piece of bone or plastic that your strings rest on at the headstock end of the fingerboard; it has small notches cut in it for each string. If the nut is too high, you will have a much harder time pressing down the strings, especially in the first couple of frets. One good test of whether your nut is too high is to put a capo at the first fret (for a full explanation of the capo, see the last question in this chapter). If your guitar feels much easier to play with the capo, your nut probably needs to be lowered, which the repair shop accomplishes with a little filing or sanding. Sometimes strings can get caught in the nut slots, which causes tuning problems and can also be fixed with some quick filing.

The **saddle** is the piece of bone or plastic (or metal on an electric) that the strings rest on at the other end of the guitar—on the bridge. Repairers often raise (or **shim**) the saddle a little bit to fix a buzz, and sand it down a little bit to lower the action. It's important that the saddle be at a height where it *can* be raised or lowered; a saddle that is teetering too high or has been ground down very low doesn't give the repairer much room for adjusting anything and is a red flag for a big problem. Other common adjustments to the saddle include filing it to improve the intonation (i.e., to make it play more in tune all the way up the neck) and smoothing out a sharp spot that causes the same string to break repeatedly.

The **truss rod** is a metal rod that runs through the middle of the neck of almost all steel-string guitars and can be adjusted to keep the neck straight. Adjustments are made either through the soundhole or beneath a small cover plate on the headstock, with small turns of an

Allen wrench. While it might be tempting to try adjusting the truss rod yourself, don't do it unless you really know what you are doing and why you are doing it. It is far too easy to misdiagnose the problem (maybe the truss rod is fine and something else is out of whack) or to turn the truss rod too far or in the wrong direction.

Like any other kind of maintenance, guitar setup is an ongoing process. Not only does your guitar change over time, but you do too, and a new development in your playing style might alter your setup preferences. Switching to heavier or lighter strings may necessitate some setup adjustments. If you want to play slide, your action might need to be a tad higher to get a decent sound. If you start tuning down the

Adjusting the truss rod with an Allen wrench.

bass strings a lot for alternate tunings, you may find that the strings buzz too much and the saddle needs to be raised on the bass side. And so on. The way to keep up with all these changes is to cultivate a relationship with a good repairer and to take your guitar in for periodic maintenance, just as you do your car.

At the top of any list of accessories has got to be strings. Without them, your guitar might look nice but will be pretty darn quiet, and you will want to keep an extra set on hand for when they break or go

Aside from my guitar itself, what pieces of equipment will I need?

dead. To set those strings ringing, you'll need some picks, unless you plan to play with your right-hand fingers. And to help you keep the strings in tune, you will want some sort of tuning device; these days, electronic tuners are inexpensive and ubiquitous, although a tuning fork will also do the trick. If your guitar didn't come with some sort of case or bag, you should get one; you could get by without it, but you are asking for dings and trouble if you are planning to take your ax with you anywhere. And where else are you going to put all the other accessories that you are now accumulating?

Optional, but very handy, is a **string winder**, a gizmo that spins your tuning pegs much more quickly than your fingers can and

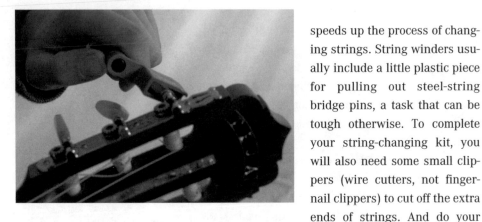

A string winder
speeds up string
changes
considerably.

A plethora of picks.

speeds up the process of changing strings. String winders usually include a little plastic piece for pulling out steel-string bridge pins, a task that can be tough otherwise. To complete your string-changing kit, you will also need some small clippers (wire cutters, not fingernail clippers) to cut off the extra ends of strings. And do your guitar a favor and throw in a nice 100-percent cotton cloth for periodic wipe-downs of the strings and body. All of the items just mentioned will be discussed in more detail in the remainder of this chapter.

You may want to use a strap to hold your guitar in position—you definitely need one if you want to play standing up. On an acoustic guitar, you may have to get a repair shop to install an **endpin** or **strap button** for attaching the strap on the butt of the guitar (all electrics, and many acoustics, come with endpins already installed). On an acoustic guitar, the other end of the strap can tie onto the headstock, or you can get a strap button installed where the neck meets the body so your strap fits snugly over your shoulders. Classical players have their own accessory for holding the guitar in the traditional playing position: a **footstool** that elevates the left leg for the guitar to lean against, or else a small frame device that sits on your leg and performs the same function but allows you to keep both feet flat on the floor.

For electric guitarists, of course, the list continues. At a bare minimum, you will need a cord (with quarter-inch jacks at both ends) and some kind of amplifier to plug it into, not to mention electrical current to make the thing run. Most likely you will also want to have an effects box of some sort, which

requires another cord and either a battery or an AC power supply. And then another box, which requires another cord and either a battery or a power supply, and then another box . . .

There are actually fewer differences than meet the eye. In fact, most of the string brands vying for your attention on the rack are made by just a handful of manufacturers, so there are greater variations in packaging and marketing than in actual string technology.

I am a little overwhelmed by all the choices of strings. What are the important differences between them?

Your guitar was designed to use either steel or nylon strings. **Steel strings** have a steel core wire, and the bottom (lowest-pitched) four strings are wound with some sort of metal as well. **Nylon strings** have a nylon core, and the bottom three strings also have metal windings. You can't really put steel strings on a guitar designed for nylon strings or vice versa—the one made for nylon strings would collapse under the much greater tension of steel strings, and the one designed for steel strings would sound pretty wimpy with nylon. The way steel and nylon strings attach to the guitar is also different, as you'll see in the next question. (The one exception to all this is a set of **ball-end nylon strings**, which can be put on a steel-string guitar, with varying sonic results.)

With steel strings, the main difference from one brand to the next is in the alloy used for the winding (brass, bronze, phosphor-bronze, etc.) and the size of the winding and core wire. Some brands are also coated to

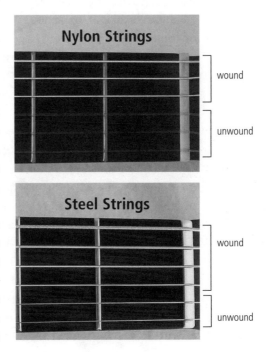

extend string life and give you a smooth feel under the fingertips. Within each brand you'll find a variety of **string gauges**—this refers to the thickness of the string, measured in hundredths of an inch. Sets are generally identified as (from thinnest to thickest) **extra-light**, **light**, **medium-light**, and **medium gauge**. (There used to be such a thing as heavy gauge, but virtually nobody uses them anymore, and for good reason—these are the kinds of strings referred to as "bridge cable." So today's medium strings are really the heaviest strings you can buy.)

The typical light-gauge set of acoustic steel strings has gauges from .012 on the first string to .054 on the sixth (the shorthand for this in guitarese is just to say the gauge of the first string, as in, "I use 12s on my Taylor"). A typical medium-gauge set goes from .013 to .056. Is that difference of .001 or .002 significant? You bet. Medium strings may pull more sound out of your guitar than lights, but they also put more tension on it—in fact, excessively heavy strings can seriously damage a guitar, so follow any guidelines you receive from a shop or manufacturer about what gauge strings to use (or not to use). Medium-gauge strings also require more muscle from you. As a rule, beginners should use light strings; Bill Purse recommends trying out **silk-and-steel strings,** which are even lighter and easier on tender fingers. As you gain strength and experience, you may want to try other gauges to find the best match for your style and your instrument. String gauge is a less complicated issue for electric guitars, because they are pretty much always strung with lights or extra-lights to facilitate string bending, and any loss in volume can be easily compensated for with the turn of a knob.

With nylon strings, you won't see designations for light and medium gauge, etc. Instead, string packages will be marked as **extra-low, low, normal, hard,** and **extra-hard tension** or something similar. Coated nylon strings are available, as are sets with wound rather than plain third strings and other special features. Some sets (both steel and nylon) are polished to reduce the squeak that inevitably happens when you slide your fingers up and down a wound string.

As you shop for strings, you will hear a lot of talk about which brands are "brighter" or "warmer" or "more brilliant." These are subjective terms, to say the least, and I would recommend ignoring them and judging for yourself how strings sound and feel. Just start with a reasonably priced set of whatever your shop recommends, and if you are so inclined, experiment with other gauges, brands, and types the next time your strings need to be changed.

Ask ten guitarists how often they change their strings, and you'll get probably as many answers: every few weeks, once a year, every couple of months, before every gig, only when strings break,

What's the best way to change strings, and how often should I do it?

never . . . Many factors affect the decision to put on a new set, from the amount you play to how hard you play to your disposable income to your laziness level to simple personal preference—new strings have a crystalline clarity that a lot of people like but others dislike. Professional musicians, who are playing constantly and need consistently high performance, tend to change strings frequently (especially if they have an endorsement deal with a string company!). There is a major physiological factor too: some people's hands produce acidic sweat that kills all the sparkle in new strings before they've even played through one song. Coated strings can help this common problem, and they will last longer regardless of what your sweat glands are like.

In other words, you have to find the string-changing schedule that works for you. Pay more attention to whether your strings still sound good and are working properly than to how much time has passed; as folk bluesman Dave Van Ronk once said, "When God wants you to change strings, He has a way of letting you know." Old strings sound dull and muffled, and they become hard to tune. And they weaken and break. If you've got a fairly old set and break a string, you may as well replace all six, because one lively new string will sound weird amidst a bunch of dead ones. Note, however, that nylon-string players often replace the wound bass strings more frequently than the unwound trebles, which last a long time. Some manufacturers address this need by packaging nylon-string sets with extra bass strings.

Now onto the matter of *how* to change strings, a pretty simple operation once you've done it a few times.

STEEL STRINGS

Step 1: Take off the old string(s). Contrary to popular belief, it won't hurt your guitar to remove all six strings at the same time if you are changing the whole set (if your guitar has an under-saddle pickup, though, this may not be advisable, as it can lead to balance problems). This is an opportunity to give your whole guitar, fingerboard and all, a good cleaning. To remove the string, you first turn the tuning machine until the string is nice and slack, and then you pull out the bridge pin. If you have a string winder with a little notch for pulling out pins, use that. Otherwise use your fingers or your string clippers, being very careful not to scratch the guitar or the pin. (Note: On electrics and some acoustic guitars, the string simply slides through a hole in the bridge rather than being held by a bridge pin. If this is true of your guitar, loosen the old strings, then cut them in half with your clippers, slide the old strings out and the new ones in, and move on to Step 3.) After the string is free on the bridge end, you can detach it from the tuning post.

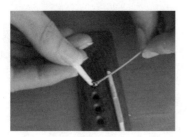

Step 2: Put a slight bend in the string down near the ball end; this will help the ball end slip into position under the bridge. Slide the ball end of the string down into the hole, followed by the bridge pin, with its hollow side facing toward the soundhole. Give a little tug on the string; the ball end should be lodged against the underside of the bridge, not hanging on the end of the bridge pin.

Step 3: Slide the other end of the string through the hole in the tuning post. Leaving a small amount of slack on the string over the fingerboard, loop the free end back around the tuning post (toward the *inside* of the headstock) and under itself, then bend it over to lock the string into position. (Note: This description assumes your steel-string guitar, like most of its

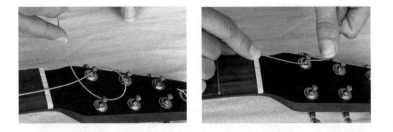

brethren, has a **solid headstock,** with the tuning posts sticking straight up and the tuning knobs on the side. A few acoustic steel-strings, however, have **slotted headstocks** similar to those found on classical guitars. If this is the case with your guitar, follow Step 3 in the nylon-string section below.)

Step 4: Tune the string up to pitch—a string winder will make the process go much more quickly. The fewer times the string wraps around the post, the better. If you've left the right amount of slack in Step 3, the string will wrap only once or twice around the post by the time it's in tune.

Step 5: With your clippers, cut off the extra string. These little sharp string ends that remain can really gouge you, so make them short. I also like to bend the ends down with the side of the clippers, just to be extra safe.

Notice on the left-hand headstock that the two rows of tuners turn in opposite directions. On the right-hand headstock, they all wind in the same direction.

NYLON STRINGS

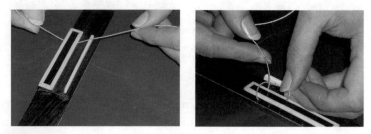

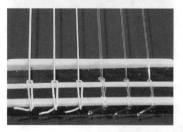

Step 1: Remove the old string by turning the tuning peg until the string is loose and can be untied easily from the tuning post and the bridge.

Step 2: Tie the string to the bridge. Classical guitar strings do not have ball ends to hold them in place, so you need to secure them with a simple loop. Push one end of the string through the hole in the bridge (if you're changing a wound string and it has one flexible end with loose windings, use this end). Loop the string back around and under itself just behind the saddle, then thread it under itself one more time at the *back* of the bridge. You can also put one more loop in the string before securing it at the back of the bridge; a common practice is to use this double loop for the unwound treble strings and a single loop for the wound basses. Clip off the extra string, leaving a short tail.

Step 3: Attach the string to the tuning post. Leaving a small amount of slack on the string over the fingerboard,

thread it through the hole in the post. Loop the free end back around and under itself, then through the loop you just made to make it secure.

Step 4: While holding the loose end of the string with one hand so the loops don't unravel, tune the string up to pitch. As with steel strings, the string should wrap around only once or twice by the time it is in tune. As you are tuning up, try to guide the string so that it wraps around the post toward the outside—this will help keep the strings away from each other.

Step 5: Using your clippers, cut off the ends of the strings down near the tuning posts.

STRETCHING

New strings take time to stretch—nylon strings may not even settle in for several days. As strings stretch, they fall in pitch, so you will need to keep tuning them back up until they stay there. You can accelerate the stretching process a little bit by giving a gentle tug on the string at around the 12th fret, then tuning back up. Do *not* yank hard on your string, though, because you'll wind up with a string that is kinked or stressed and impossible to tune.

Now the work is done, so enjoy your new strings. Fresh strings and a good polishing can give your guitar—and you—a whole new lease on life.

There are five basic types of cases offering quite a wide range of protection (from very little to practically gorillaproof) and cost (from $20 on up to more than you probably paid for your guitar).

What kinds of cases are available?

The most basic case, and the one that traditionally comes with a budget guitar, is made of
chipboard, which is like a heavier form of card-
board. Shops refer to these as **soft-shell cases**. If you
have an inexpensive guitar and only need a case to
stow it away at home and carry it around locally, a
soft-shell case will do fine. Don't expect it to
do much other than keep your guitar
from getting scratched; it offers
minimal protection from impact.

Higher-end guitars
come with hard-
shell cases.

Moving up a notch in quality
and security are plywood **hard-
shell cases**. Pricier models have thicker
wood and are arched on the top and back for better impact protection, and their latches and handles
are sturdier. Many high-quality guitars these
days come in molded plastic cases, which are a
lighter-weight alternative to plywood cases.
Whether ply or plastic, these kinds of cases will
protect your guitar from small bumps and some rough handling,
but they are not adequate for serious traveling.

At the high end are **flight cases**, which are designed
to help your guitar survive the rigors of baggage han-
dlers and the road. These are expensive, heavy duty,
and just plain heavy but are considered essential
equipment for traveling musicians with fine instruments.

By contrast, **gig bags** provide only padding for
the guitar rather than a rigid shell. In return you get
very light weight and great portability—you can
sling your guitar right over your shoulder or
carry it like a backpack. There is a huge
range in level of protection and price for
gig bags, from basic nylon exterior and
little or no padding to swanky leather
and thick foam. Gig bags are made for car-
rying your guitar around town, not for trav-

For serious
traveling: the flight
case.

eling. Since a gig bag takes up much less room than other kinds of cases, it is tempting to carry your guitar onto a plane in one of these for easy stowing in the overhead compartment. But these days, a flight attendant might very well force you to relinquish your guitar to baggage; if that happens, you are going to be very sorry you don't have a hard case.

Obviously, the quality of case you should get rises with the quality of the guitar, and the more traveling you do, the better case you will need. No matter what kind of case you choose, it should fit snugly around your guitar without putting pressure on any of its parts, and it should support the neck. The latches and the handle should be strong and reliable—believe me, you do *not* want

Guitar to go: the gig bag.

your case to open up accidentally as you are walking down the sidewalk with it. And a case should feel natural and comfortable to carry. Some heavier cases can be extremely cumbersome, and the sad truth is that more than a few musicians have injured their hands not from playing too much but from schlepping their instruments around.

In taking care of your guitar, a little common sense goes a long way. Keep your guitar in a safe place where it will not get knocked over by kids or dogs or someone fumbling for the door in the dark, and prefer-

What do I need to know about taking care of my guitar at home and away?

ably store it in a sturdy case with all the latches closed so you won't inadvertently pick up the case and deposit your guitar on the floor. If you use a guitar stand, buy a good one that will not tip over easily, and find a place for it away from foot traffic. Don't go straight from eating a plateful of greasy french fries to playing your guitar—wash your hands and save your strings. Keep jewelry, zippers, and big belt buckles away from your guitar, because all can leave scratches in the finish.

Aside from these sorts of household hazards, the most important factors in your guitar's welfare are temperature and humidity—both have a dramatic effect on the structural stability and playability of

wooden instruments. "Keep away from extremes of temperature," says Stan Werbin of Elderly Instruments in Lansing, Michigan. "I would say try to avoid prolonged exposure to temperatures under 50 or over 100 degrees Fahrenheit." That means keep your guitar out of the chilly basement and away from radiators and heating vents as well as intense direct sunlight, whether indoors or out. If you hang your guitar on the wall, avoid the outside walls of the building. An extremely common guitar killer is the trunk or back of a car, which on a sunny summer day can do serious damage within a short period of time. Imagine yourself in the guitar's position; only leave your guitar in places where you yourself would be comfortable.

Secure those latches before you hit the road.

Humidity is a subtler though no less important consideration. Your regional climate is a major variable—a guitarist in bone-dry Arizona faces different issues from someone in sticky Florida—although many places experience high humidity on muggy summer days and low humidity during the winter when central heating dries out the indoor air. "Always keep your guitar well humidified," says Werbin. "At home, if possible, use a house or room humidifier that keeps the humidity between 40 and 50 percent. Don't trust cheap gauges to measure humidity, since they are notoriously inaccurate." If your room or house is too dry, or if you are going away from home for an extended period of time, a **soundhole humidifier** (available at music stores) will keep your guitar in good shape, although you need to be careful not to overhumidify or spill water on it. Watch your instrument: if your guitar is too dry, the top may sink and the strings may start to buzz on the higher frets, while excessive humidity may make the top bulge out and the action too high. For high humidity, a room dehumidifier or else a silica gel pack in the case will keep moisture in the normal range.

Pad the headstock before you fly.

A lot of these problems are alleviated, or at least lessened, by keeping your guitar in a good hard-shell case, which acts as a buffer against the environment. If you transport your instrument through subzero weather and then bring it inside a toasty house, leave the guitar in its case for a few minutes to warm up slowly. If you open it right away, you might be greeted with an ugly crack in the finish.

A good case, of course, also protects your guitar from many of the hazards of traveling. That is, except human ones—keep your guitar with you as much as possible to avoid theft.

Airline travel is a source of major anxiety for musicians, and with good reason, given all the instruments that are battered, cracked, stolen, and lost every day somewhere between the plane and baggage claim. Try to carry your guitar on board with you, but don't be surprised if you are intercepted by a flight attendant. Be polite but firm in pointing out that your guitar will fit in the overhead bin (and hope that this is, in fact, true!); minimize your other carry-ons so that you don't look like a space hog. Even if you are forced to hand over your guitar (and on little commuter planes you have no choice), you are probably better off having checked it at the gate, where it doesn't have to negotiate the baggage maze. Ask to pick it up at the other end right when you get off the plane, although regulations may prevent you from doing this.

The odds of your guitar emerging intact from the baggage hold are greatly increased by a heavy-duty case. No matter what type of case you have, loosen the strings before you go on board (this might keep the peghead from snapping off if your case takes a big hit) and pack some T-shirts or other soft clothes under and on top of the peghead, just to give it extra support.

Finally, a word about cleaning your guitar. For most everyday dirt, a simple wipe with a soft chamois cloth or old cotton T-shirt is all you need. Wiping off your strings after each playing session will lengthen their life. For more stubborn dirt on the body of the guitar, first try breathing a little moisture onto the dirty spot and then wiping it off; if that doesn't work, use one of the guitar cleaners available at the music store. Over time, grime will build up on your fingerboard. Once in a while (maybe once a year), when you are changing strings, you can gently clean the fingerboard with very fine (0000 grade) steel wool. Add a tiny dab of lemon oil if you like, wipe off any excess, and your guitar is ready to go.

What is the difference between using a flatpick, fingerpicks, and your plain old fingers?

Let's sort out the terms first, because they can be baffling. First we have the triangular-shaped **flatpick**, also known simply as a **pick** or (in millions of dusty old method books) as a **plectrum**. No matter what word you use, you hold a flatpick between your thumb and index finger and strike the strings with it. Flatpicks are the driving force in all sorts of guitar music, but, confusingly enough, people often use the term **flatpicking** to refer specifically to bluegrass guitar technique.

Fingerpicks are metal or plastic extensions for your index, middle, ring, and sometimes pinky fingers that give them a lot more power in attacking the strings. They are almost always accompanied by a **thumbpick**, which similarly turbocharges the thumb. (A thumbpick is not, however, always accompanied by fingerpicks—many players, from Chet Atkins on down, use a thumbpick and bare fingers.) Fingerpicks find their most common use in country blues and folk. Again, just for a little confusion, **fingerpicking** doesn't necessarily mean using fingerpicks—it just means using your fingers instead of a flatpick. (Sorry! I didn't come up with these terms.) **Fingerstyle** is used pretty much interchangeably with *fingerpicking*.

Each of these little devices has its pros and cons. The flatpick is a rhythm machine, great for strumming and percussive grooves and for getting lots of noise out of your guitar, plus it is the tool of choice for most modern lead-guitar styles. The main limitation of the flatpick is that it has only one point of contact with the strings; by contrast, if you use your fingers, you can have four or even five appendages working on different strings simultaneously. So the finger-style approach opens up a lot of technical and musical possibilities, although by dropping the pick you give up a lot of easily accessible volume and power. You can develop those things playing fingerstyle, but it takes considerably more finesse.

Take your pick: a flatpick (top) and thumb- and fingerpicks.

Playing with fingerpicks feels quite different from using your bare fingers. With fingerpicks, your fingers are further away from the strings. You get lots of volume—in fact, maybe too much, because it is hard to control the clatter and get a good tone. If you go with the bare digits, you have yet more choices: you can maintain longish fingernails (or apply artificial nails), as most nylon-string players and many steel-string fingerpickers do, or you can simply use the pads of your fingertips.

As you can see, there are quite a few options when it comes to something as basic as deciding how to hit the string—that's one of the keys to the guitar's versatility. Many guitarists wind up using more than one technique or develop a hybrid (a common one being **pick and fingers**—holding a flatpick and then fingerpicking with the middle and ring fingers). The good news is that experimenting with various types of picks is cheap and fun. Your choices include not only flatpicks vs. fingerpicks vs. no picks but all the many materials and gauges (thicknesses) of picks available today. Trying different possibilities is certainly a lot easier on the wallet than buying different guitars!

What is a capo, and how do you use one?

A **capo** is a slick little device that presses down all six strings of the guitar at whatever fret you choose. There are several designs, from simple elastic bands that wrap around the neck to various ways of clamping and holding a bar down across the fingerboard (in a pinch, you can even try the traditional homemade version with a pencil and a thick rubber band!). Guitarists will go to their graves arguing for the inherent superiority of one model over another, but no matter—all capos perform the same basic function.

And that function is to raise the pitch of all the strings by the same amount without your needing to retune them. If you attach the capo at the first fret, for instance, your open strings now ring a **half step** (the interval of one fret) higher in pitch. If the capo is at the second fret, all the strings are a **whole step** (two frets) higher—your normal tuning of E A D G B E is now magically raised to F♯B E A C♯ F♯. And so on up the neck.

So why would you want to clamp such a thing on your unsuspecting guitar? For several very good reasons. The main one is to accommodate the range of your singing voice. Let's say you are singing a song in the key of A and accompanying yourself with A, D, and E chords, but the melody is a bit low for your voice. You could put a capo at the second fret, hold those same chord fingerings, and sing comfortably, because the melody is now a whole step higher. You are actually playing in the key of B—the capo has raised your A to B, your D to E, and your E to F♯, even

This capo is holding down all the strings at the second fret.

if you don't know how to play an F♯ chord on your own! Neat trick, eh?

Take a look at the chart on page 61, which shows what chords you get when you play the five most common open chords with a capo at various positions up the neck. Only the first seven frets are listed, because capos are rarely used higher than that.

No capo	Fret 1	2	3	4	5	6	7
A	A♯/B♭	B	C	C♯/D♭	D	D♯/E♭	E
C	C♯/D♭	D	D♯/E♭	E	F	F♯/G♭	G
D	D♯/E♭	E	F	F♯/G♭	G	G♯/A♭	A
E	F	F♯/G♭	G	G♯/A♭	A	A♯/B♭	B
G	G♯/A♭	A	A♯/B♭	B	C	C♯/D♭	D

All those sharps (♯) and flats (♭) may make your eyes a little bleary, but remember that as far as your fingers are concerned, you are still playing the five familiar chords in the first column; the capo does the work of transforming them into the other chords listed.

In addition to adjusting the key to make your voice or someone else's more comfortable, you might use a capo to play along with another instrument. Let's say your pal likes to sing and play a song in the dreaded key of F—you could capo at the first fret and play a nice, easy E fingering. Capos are used in a lot of recorded music, so strapping one on might also help you play along with a CD.

Finally, the capo gives you the option to play the *same* chords at a different place on the neck and therefore get a different sound. An example: You could play G, C, and D chords without the capo in the usual way, but you could also put a capo at the fifth fret and then play D, G, and A fingerings that will *sound* as G, C, and D. Chord positions up the neck like this have a distinctive flavor—just think of the sweet little guitar part in "Here Comes the Sun," which we owe not only to George Harrison but to his capo (he capos at the fifth fret and plays D fingerings that sound in the key of G).

Finally, there is one fringe benefit to the capo for beginners: it tends to make your guitar's action a tad lower, especially when you capo on the first few frets, so the strings become a little easier to play. Nothing wrong with easing up on the finger calisthenics from time to time.

GETTING IN TUNE AND GETTING STARTED

There are two paths to getting your guitar in tune—using a tuning device and using your ears—and both are essential. For a beginner, a device like an electronic tuner is a godsend: it helps you over the initial hurdle of getting in correct tune, and it also initiates the longer and no less important process of training your ears to know instinctively when a string is or is not quite in tune.

What's the best way to tune my guitar?

Before we run through a few good methods and tools for tuning, let's check the notes that we are actually tuning the strings to. The notes of **standard tuning** on the guitar are, from the lowest-pitched string to the highest:

String	6	5	4	3	2	1
Note	E	A	D	G	B	E

The way you tune the strings, of course, is by turning your **tuning pegs** (which are, by the way, also referred to as **gears**, **tuning machines**, or just plain **tuners**); one direction raises the pitch, the other lowers it. No matter what tuning method you use, always tune a string *up* to the target pitch—the tuning will be more stable that way.

What's on top?

One endless source of confusion is all the ways people refer to their strings (high, low, top, bottom, first, sixth . . .). Here's a rundown of seven ways to describe those six strings of yours.

E	A	D	G	B	E
Sixth	Fifth	Fourth	Third	Second	First
Thickest	. . . .				Thinnest
Lowest pitch	. . . .				Highest pitch
Bottom	. . . .				Top
Low E	. . . .				High E
Bass	. . . .				Treble
Closest to ceiling	. . . .				Closest to floor

The important thing to remember is that most of these terms refer to the pitch. That is, your "high E" or "top" string is the highest-pitched one, and your "low E" or "bottom" string is the lowest-pitched one. That makes sense, as long you don't get hung up on the fact that the "high" or "top" string is actually the lowest one in vertical space (i.e., closest to the floor), while the "low" or "bottom" string is closest to the ceiling.

There is one other string-related oddity you should know about. Tunings are always listed from the lowest-pitched string to the highest (E A D G B D), yet the strings are numbered from the highest-pitched (1) to the lowest (6).

If you can just commit these things to memory, as counterintuitive as they may seem, you'll save yourself a lot of headaches while reading lesson books or communicating with other guitarists.

That means if the string is tuned a little too high, you should drop it *below* the note you want and then raise it slowly back up.

ELECTRONIC TUNERS

These battery-powered devices listen to the sound of an individual string ringing and indicate on a meter of some sort (usually lights or a needle) whether the note is higher than, lower than, or right on the desired pitch. Electronic tuners pick up the sound through either a small built-in microphone or a direct feed from an electronic pickup—you plug your guitar cord right into the tuner. Some models attach temporarily onto the body or headstock of the guitar and "read" the pitch from the vibrations rather than from the air, which works much better than a mic in a noisy room. The exact way that tuners function varies from model to model—on some, you need to flick a switch to tell the tuner which string you're tuning, while "hands-off" models take care of that automatically. The simplest guitar tuners read only the notes in standard tuning; more expensive **chromatic tuners** can read any note, which is a handy function if you ever get into alternate tunings or want to check your tuning while using a capo.

These days, for the truly wired guitarist, there are software tuners that function similarly to stand-alone electronic tuners—you plug into your computer to check your tuning. These programs have the advantage of being able to play notes through MIDI files, and some offer sophisticated functions for alternate tunings.

Electronic tuners are found in just about everyone's guitar case—they're cheap and easy to use, and on stage or in some other noisy environment, they provide just about the only feasible way to tune. Pitch pipes, which used to be standard guitar-case accessories before electronic tuners, can go out of tune themselves, and besides, they don't tell you whether you are in tune or not. The one caveat about using an electronic tuner is that you should not shut off your ears. "It is easy to be kind of mindless and just look at it—'Oh, it's in the middle, so it must be in tune,' and move on to the next string without actually getting involved in the process," says Carol McComb. "You need to listen if you're trying to develop your ears. Tuners are very good biofeedback tools, if you pay attention to them and listen to the note and think, 'Do I think this is in tune? And does the machine think this is in tune?'"

This basic tuner reads the notes of standard tuning.

Keep in mind that tuners show only a very small variation above and below the target note. So if your string is way off, the tuner won't give you a useful reading. You have to get the string in the neighborhood of the correct note, then fine-tune it using the tuner. For that reason, it's a good idea to have a tuning fork even if you've got an electronic tuner—it will give you a note you can hear and sing for getting in the ballpark of the correct pitch.

A tuning fork held against the bridge produces a clear, loud tone.

TUNING FORK

If you are not using an electronic tuner, you will be mostly relying on your ears and fingers to tune up your guitar. But unless you are blessed with perfect pitch (i.e., you can sing a dead-on A note out of the blue), you will need some way of knowing that at least one of your strings is in correct tune. Once you have that, you can tune all the others in relation to that one string.

The **tuning fork** is one simple, portable tool for finding that reference note. You just hold it by the stem down near the knob end, knock the prongs against something hard like a guitar case (not, please, your guitar), then, while letting the prongs vibrate, rest the knob on the top or bridge of your guitar, which will produce a clear, loud tone. Most guitarists use an E tuning fork, which matches the open first string; another option is **A 440** (440 hertz, that is), which is considered the standard reference pitch for all music and corresponds to the note at the fifth fret on your first string. After you tune one string correctly, follow the fretted-notes method below to tune the other strings.

If you have trouble hearing whether the string is higher or lower than the pitch of the tuning fork, try singing or humming the two notes. The higher note will feel higher in your throat.

PIANO
You can get all six of the pitches you need from a piano, as shown in the diagram. I would recommend, however, using a piano for only one reference pitch—just hit an A on the piano and tune your fifth string to it. Then tune up all the other strings in relation to each other, away from the piano. That way, you won't get thrown off if the other piano keys are slightly out of tune, and besides, even under the best circumstances, it is difficult to get a guitar and a piano to sound exactly in tune with each other.

FRETTED NOTES
Here is the simplest way to tune up without an electronic tuner. First, you should get a reference note from a tuning fork, a piano, or another instrument. Let's begin here by tuning your first string to an E note, but you could start with any of the other strings.

As you may have noticed, your first string is not the only one tuned to E—your sixth string is too, so let's go to that one next. These strings are tuned in **octaves**, which are simply occurrences of the same note at different frequencies. The sixth-string E is two octaves lower than the first-string E. It's pretty easy to hear when octaves are in tune, so play the first and sixth strings back to back and adjust the sixth to match the first. (For an even slicker way to tune the sixth string to the first, see the harmonics section below.)

Now onto the other strings. When your guitar is in tune, with one exception, each open string matches the note you get at the fifth fret on the string below it in pitch. So, for example, the fifth string matches the note on the fifth fret of the sixth string. The exception is that the second string matches the note on the *fourth* fret of the third string. Take a look at the fingerboard diagram and you'll see how this pattern goes.

So let's use this information. Once your sixth string is in tune, you want to play it at the fifth fret and match the open fifth string to that A note. Does the fifth string sound higher or lower? If it's lower (**flat**), raise the pitch by tightening the tuning peg slightly and then

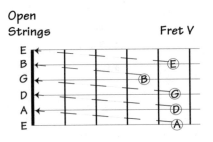

rechecking the note. If it's higher (**sharp**), loosen the string by turning the tuning peg in the other direction. If you are not sure which way you need to go, try moving up and down the frets on the sixth string: if, when you play the sixth string at frets one through four, it sounds like the note is closer to the open fifth string, then you need to tune the fifth string higher; if, when you play the sixth string at fret six or higher, the pitch sounds closer to the fifth string, then you need to tune down.

Follow the same procedure for all the other strings. The fifth fret of the fifth string matches the open fourth string, the fifth fret of the fourth string matches the open third string, the *fourth* fret of the third string matches the open second string, and if all has gone according to plan, the fifth fret of the second string now matches the already-tuned first string. If not, you need to go back and recheck the whole chain of tuning, starting with your reference note and string.

When two strings are in tune, the fretted note and the open string are in **unison**—the pitch is the same. When two strings are close to the same pitch but not quite, you will (if you listen very closely) hear something usually referred to as beats—a subtle pulsing that results from the way the sound waves rub against each other. When the two notes are in unison, the beating disappears—it sounds smooth and even. Try listening for these beats and using them to help you home in on the right note.

OCTAVE CHECK

Octaves provide a good way to check the results of the fretted-notes method. Not only do you have E notes on the open first and sixth strings, but you have one on the second fret of the fourth string as well. So you can check that all these notes sound in tune with each other, and do the same thing for other notes and other strings.

Here is a series of octaves that you can check for each open string.

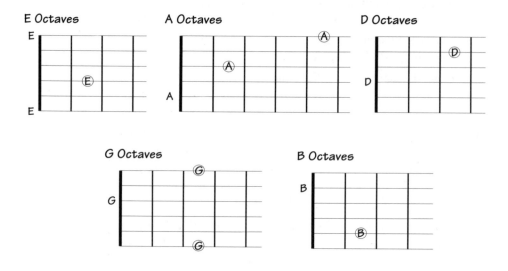

HARMONICS CHECK

Here is one last way to check your tuning. A **harmonic** is that nice, chiming tone you get by lightly touching a string directly above a fret (not pressing it down against the fingerboard) and picking it with your other hand. It's a magical sound, and it can be useful for fine-tuning your strings. Here are some harmonics and the fretted notes you can check them against.

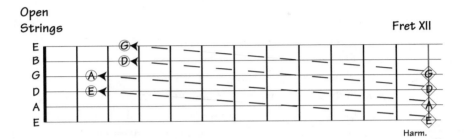

Last but not least, try the one at right. It's harder to get fifth-fret harmonics to ring than 12th-fret ones, but keep micro-adjusting the placement of your finger on the string and eventually you'll find the sweet spot. As mentioned above, if you tune your first string to a tuning fork, you can use this harmonic to tune the sixth string, then use the fretted-notes method to tune strings five, four, three, and two.

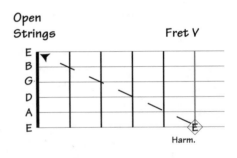

If you try out a few of these tuning methods, you'll find that some are easier for you to hear and use than others—it's an individual thing. Start with an electronic tuner; and when you're comfortable with that, try tuning one string with the tuner and then the rest by ear with the fretted-notes method. Your ears, after all, do not require batteries, and training them well is an investment that will pay off as long as you play music.

This, unfortunately, is one of those rites of passage for everyone learning the guitar—especially the steel-string variety. Your fingertips, which have led a pretty cushy life to date, suddenly find themselves having to

Will these painful ruts across my fingertips ever go away?

press against thin wires, sometimes for hours at a time, and they will complain bitterly about their new assignment. But yes, the pain will diminish as your fingers toughen up and calluses develop, probably in a matter of weeks or a few months, so hang in there. In the future, you may go through this experience again if you take a hiatus from the guitar or if you significantly notch up the time and intensity of your playing, but it probably won't hurt as much as developing your first set of calluses.

There are a few tips that might ease the pain in the meantime. One is using lighter-gauge strings: lights are much softer to press down than mediums, and silk-and-steels are even softer still. Coated strings, though more expensive, also do not dig into your fingertips as hard as regular strings do. Another consideration is action: if your strings are higher off the fingerboard than they need to be, some inexpensive adjustments might really help (see the setup discussion in Equipment Basics).

Pace yourself while you play, too. Short, daily practice sessions are better for building calluses than one marathon a week. Usually what hurts the most is holding the same chords down for very long periods of time, so switching over to a different song or exercise might give you some relief. Don't push yourself too hard, and definitely give it a rest if you feel pain in your hand, wrist, or arm, which could be a sign of a more serious problem.

As a guitar player, you need to be more careful about your fingers than you probably were in the past. Keep harsh solvents and cleaners away from your skin—use rubber gloves. Also, don't play guitar when your fingertips are waterlogged. Wear rubber gloves while you do the dishes, or else just give your fingers time to dry and harden before you pick up the guitar. All these measures help protect your picking-hand fingernails, too, if you are using those.

As the skin toughens, some people find that their calluses get so thick that they actually catch on the strings and even break off. A little filing with an emery board can help smooth the calluses out, and if your fingertips get dry and cracked, soaking them in Vaseline or something similar (overnight, with a Band-Aid covering them) can be soothing. Just make sure they're not still greased up when you play again.

These kinds of difficulties are most easily straight-ened out in person, with a teacher looking at exactly how your fingers are falling on your guitar. But there are some common problems that beginners face, so here are a few ideas.

In some chord positions, my fingers don't "fit" right, or else I can't get all the strings to ring out. Any trouble-shooting tips?

First, to diagnose your precise trouble spot, hold down the chord in question and play the strings one at a time, listening for which one is thumping rather than ringing out. Make sure that your finger is pressing the string down just *behind* the fret (toward the tuners), rather than directly over the fret or in the middle between two frets. Use just enough force to hold the string down firmly—don't mash it against the fingerboard.

Another likely cause of muted strings is that one of your other fingers is in the way. In the basic C fin-gering below, for instance, it is very easy to inadver-tently mute the fourth string by leaning your ring finger (which is playing the third fret of the fifth string) against it. If you straighten that finger up, the fourth string will start ringing again. Same goes with the G chord: if the fourth string is muted, the finger holding the fifth string at the second fret is probably the culprit. And with a D, you might be silencing the first string by leaning your ring finger against it, as shown in the photo. (If you are not sure how to read these chord diagrams, see page 89.)

The ring finger in this D chord is falling too flat and muting the first string.

C
x32010

G
320004

D
xx0132

When beginners talk about their fingers not "fitting," chances are they are referring to the A chord—specifically the fingering with the index, middle, and ring fingers all in a row:

A
x01230

Some people's fingers are so thick (or the string spacing on the guitar is so narrow relative to the size of their fingers) that they just won't fit like this without pushing one of the fingers practically back to the first fret. In this situation, an alternate fingering might help, like this A position with the index tucked between your middle and ring fingers:

My thin fingers line up in a row without difficulty, but I prefer this fingering anyway because it gives me a nice pivot for going to the D chord—that is, my first finger can stay in place at the second fret of the third string for both chords.

There are also two- and one-finger options for the A that do the trick for some people. In the version at left below, your index finger takes care of two strings and your middle finger grabs one. In the version at right, you lay your index finger down across all three strings. This position can come in very handy, but it requires more strength than the others, and some people's index finger joints just won't bend to get out of the way of the first string.

As you can see from these examples, there are various ways to finger chords, and different options will be more efficient in different situations or simply feel better for different fingers. Experienced guitarists know a few ways of grabbing a chord, which they can pull out of their bag of tricks as needed.

Practice. Practice. And did I mention practice?

How can I train my fingers to go smoothly from one chord to another?

Seriously, if there is one thing that guitar teachers agree on, it is that we learn most effectively by isolating a small problem, creating a simple exercise, and repeating and repeating and repeating it, as slowly as we need to, until we get it right. This is a truth known instinctively by my toddler son, I noticed recently; when he is trying to memorize the name of something, he points to one thing and then the other, one thing and then the other, one thing and then the other, asking me to repeat the two words sometimes ten or 15 times until he's got it—then he won't ask again. The guitar equivalent of this is, if you are having trouble going from a G chord to a C, slow it down and do that single change over and over until you think you are going to go out of your tree—and at that point you will have it.

Some other tips:

Visualize the chord shapes. "What slows people down is that they move one finger at a time instead of moving into the whole shape at once," says Bill Purse. "If you move the first finger, then the second, then the third, you are not going to get it." As a way to burn the whole chord shape in your memory, Carol McComb recommends holding the shape, scrambling your fingers, holding the shape, scrambling your fingers, etc., until your fingers spring into action the instant you see or think "D." The more your instincts take over, the less you have to look at your fingers, which always slows you down.

Aim for the bass string (the lowest note in the chord) first, because that is the one you hit first when you strum. When you are moving to a G, for instance, if you get your finger down on the third fret of the sixth string quickly, that will buy you some time to get your other fingers in place. Every split second helps.

Look for places where you can leave a finger in the same place during a chord change, or maybe slide it just one fret, rather than lifting all your fingers off the fingerboard and replanting them. For instance, if you play the A fingering below, you can slide the third finger up a fret to play the D fingering at right. That'll keep you anchored during the move.

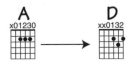

Finally, make sure you are keeping a steady tempo rather than pausing and then lurching ahead at the chord change. A metronome can help keep you honest; set the click as slow as you need to in order to play evenly and smoothly through the change, then speed up the tempo in small increments.

Is it best to focus on either rhythm or lead guitar, or to learn both?

In a band, lead guitarists seem to get the spotlight and the glory, while rhythm players chunka-chunk away in the background. Many beginners are, naturally enough, in a hurry to learn all those cool, gravity-defying lead licks, but the truth is that rhythm is the essential starting point for guitar. No band can function without a solid rhythm player; if the lead player is at home with the flu, the party goes on. As Jimmy Tomasello puts it, "The world is full of half-ass lead guitar players who can't play 12-bar rhythm in B♭. All the music comes from the chords and the harmony and keeping time. If you can't keep time, no one will want to hear what you have to say."

On the other hand, there is a lot to be said for early exposure to playing simple melodies and lead as you work on your rhythm basics. Many teachers point out that there is a big gender gap here— girls and women tend to stick with rhythm and never explore lead, while guys make that leap early and easily. "I find that especially women are much less intimidated if they learn notes and chords at the same time," says Marcy Marxer. "It doesn't matter if they are not aiming for, say, flatpicking or jazz [lead styles]. It just helps people have an overall concept of the guitar, and it sounds good." Marxer has ways of introducing lead to even rank beginners: they learn a couple of chords, and then she shows them how they can jam over those chords using just one note, by varying the rhythm. This may not be fancy but it is real improvisation, and it helps to demystify the world of lead guitar.

Players who focus only on rhythm and accompaniment often orient themselves on the guitar entirely with visual chord shapes— clusters of fingers on frets. Learning to play simple melodies and lead lines opens the door to understanding the individual notes on the fingerboard; even if you continue to focus on accompaniment, knowledge of the notes directly feeds into new chords and new sounds. As Cathy Fink puts it, learning rhythm and lead simultaneously is "conceptually the same thing as learning to play by ear and learning to read notes at the same time." The more skills you have, the more options and possibilities will open up on your guitar.

There are a lot of variables embedded in this seemingly simple question about how best to ring those strings. First of all, what kind of guitar are you using?

Is it better to start off playing with a pick or your fingers?

Fingers are usually the tool of choice for nylon-string instruments, and certain styles (e.g., classical and flamenco) really require the dexterity of five digits. Picks also shred nylon strings more easily and quickly than your fingertips or nails; conversely, nylon strings are pretty gentle on your nails (steel strings can chew them up in no time). There *are* nylon-string pick players out there, and even some red-hot ones, but if you play a nylon-string and are looking for a general guideline, it is: use your fingers.

With steel-string guitars, as noted in last chapter's discussion of flatpicks and fingerpicks, it's a wide-open field. With certain styles (bluegrass and rock, for instance), the flatpick rules, so if that is where you are headed with your music, grab a pick and go for it. If you are like most beginners, though, you aren't exactly sure what type of music you are ultimately going to play, and both fingerstyle and flatpicking approaches might be useful for you. Which leads us back to the original question: which is best to start with?

Many guitar teachers choose to start beginners with a pick, but it's not the only way.

Guitar teachers will give you different answers. A pick gives you a single point of attack (rather than multiple digits to train) and an easy tool for strumming, so many teachers start off beginners that way. Others prefer to teach strumming as a brush across the strings with the thumb—this is a very natural motion, in some ways simpler than figuring out how to hold a pick and wield it effectively. Other teachers put the question aside for the very early stages. "Most of the focus in my beginning classes is on getting the

left hand or fretting hand to work," says Mark Dvorak. "Once we get a few chords together with some simple strumming, we then begin exploring different ways of making guitar sounds with our right hand."

The truth is that you can't go wrong starting with either finger-style or flatpicking—if you have a good teacher, his or her preferred method will get you up and playing, and you can always try other techniques later. If you have a strong desire to learn a particular style, by all means find out how that music is conventionally played and go that route. If you don't have a particularly strong stylistic direction or teacher to lead you, you might want to expose yourself to a little of both techniques. Strumming with a pick and playing fingerstyle are very different in terms of sounds and motions, and experimenting with both is a good education for your hands and might help you understand where you want to go next on the guitar. Like learning a little bit of a foreign language at a young age, the experience of trying several approaches will make it easier for you to broaden your guitar horizons even years down the road.

How can I get barre chords to ring out clearly?

As you ask the question, thousands of other beginners are nodding their heads emphatically, thinking, "Yeah, how *do* you do that?" **Barre chords**—those chord positions in which one of your fingers (usually the index) lies flat across several or all of the strings and heroically presses them down—have the reputation of being the single biggest hurdle that you have to clear in learning to play, and veteran players often remember their first clean F barre chord as a historic victory. But the truth is, players learn to tackle the dreaded barre chord every day, and contrary to popular belief, they don't all have Olympian finger muscles. You need some finger strength, it's true, but what you need even more is good technique—hands and arms placed correctly and energy used efficiently.

A series of building blocks prepares you for understanding barre chords and playing them clearly, which is why most guitar teachers introduce them well into the lesson plan. "There's a time for it," says Bill Purse. "You'll know when you're ready. You've got to get a whole series of chords in first position under your belt first. At that point you will have built up enough strength in the fingers." He also drills students on the notes on the fifth and sixth strings, which are the **root notes** of the basic barre chord forms and therefore tell you the name of the chord you're playing.

Cathy Fink uses the analogy of the capo to help players understand what's going on in a barre chord. "After people know their E chord or their A minor or their A chords, and they understand the use of the capo—how moving the capo up and down the neck changes what chords they're playing or what key they're playing in—then we can demonstrate barre chords and how they work pretty simply." For instance, play an E chord with this alternate fingering, using your middle, ring, and pinky fingers:

Your index finger becomes available to take on the role of the capo. You can move the E chord up a fret, with your first finger barring the whole first fret:

And then you can keep moving that up, just as you might move the capo into different positions on the neck. "I think once people use their imagination that the finger is like a fake capo," says Fink, "it just snaps right into place how barre chords really work."

So much for the conceptual talk, you're probably thinking. How about getting rid of that depressing *thunk* you get when you try a barre chord? Well, here are some troubleshooting tips:

* As with any chord, make sure you are pressing down the string right next to the fret—you always get a cleaner sound this way.

* Make sure all the strings are being pressed down by the fleshy

Good thumb position—in the middle of the neck—is key for a clean barre chord.

parts of your barre finger, not stuck in a groove at the joint. A slight move up or down can get the string out of this little rut in your finger, which is bound to mute it.

* Don't overextend your first finger above the neck (it shouldn't poke above the fingerboard).

* Don't press too hard. "There's a point where it doesn't return on the quality of the chord," says Bill Purse. Concentrate instead on finger position.

* Try adjusting your left arm's position; instead of tucking your elbow in by your side, rotate it out slightly to gain a bit more leverage.

* Remember that in a typical barre chord, your barre finger is only pressing down a few of the strings, so focus your efforts on those strings and don't worry about the others.

* Make sure your thumb is well behind the neck. "If it creeps around at all, you can't put your index finger across in a straight line," says Carol McComb. "The further around your thumb reaches, the more you are inclined to bend your index finger." And use your thumb to support the effort of your finger.

* And finally, as with learning any new skill, take it slowly, starting with just a few minutes at a time. You can also ease into the full six-string barre chord by playing partial barre chords first—for instance, this four-string G fingering followed by the five-string one and finally the six-string version.

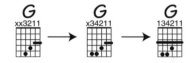

A little bit of practice, increasing gradually over successive days/week/months, will get you there eventually.

In the meantime, maybe you can psych yourself up by following the example of Cathy Fink. "I started playing guitar when I was 12, and I had a wacky teacher who thought it was important to learn barre chords early on, even though no one else did," she recalls. "So within the first six months of learning guitar I was playing barre chords. I just didn't know that they were supposed to be so hard, and so they never have been."

Singing and playing simultaneously can seem, at first, a little like rubbing your belly and tapping your head at the same time (or was that rubbing your head and tapping your belly?). You need to coordinate your two hands to keep a steady rhythm on the guitar and then keep track of the melody, which moves at a different pace. On top of all that, you're trying to keep your voice on pitch and remember the words!

So how do you teach yourself to do this kind of multitasking? By simplifying and practicing the individual components, then putting them all together. First of all, choose a song that comes very easily and naturally to you—a song that is comfortable to sing, has familiar words, and uses a small number of simple chords that don't change too frequently. Save that favorite song with the tricky chord positions and fast changes for later. In magazines and books and on the Web, you'll find arrangements of pop songs with simplified chords and accompaniment parts, which might work well for this purpose. Simply choosing an accessible song might be enough to get you up and running, but if not, read on.

Mark Dvorak recommends building the song literally from the ground up. "A good approach is to chant the words," he says. "That is, put the syllables where you think they belong while you strum or pick your guitar arrangement. Slower is better, as it gives you time to hear what's supposed to happen.

"If it's still difficult, try simplifying the accompaniment. If you work your way through the progression strumming only the first beat of each measure, you'll be reducing the job to some pretty basic terms. You can also try chanting and strumming with a friend or a small group. Try it together, or experiment with one person only chanting and not strumming. Have someone else only strum and not chant. The others will have strong models of each as they try to do both."

From there, you can add in elements one at a time—the melody, a steady strum, then a more elaborate accompaniment part. Soon you will be ready to serenade your family, your friends, your dog, or just the four walls of your room. There's nothing quite like being able to play a complete song like that, breathing and singing and strumming it into life.

THE LEARNING PROCESS

Let's start with some of the *least* effective ways to practice. Noodling on the guitar while kicking back on the couch and watching TV may be more fun than

What's the most effective way to practice?

watching TV by itself, but it'll drive anyone else in the room crazy, and it won't do much for your chops. Playing the same handful of songs you know really well time and time again won't help you progress either—in fact, it can make you even less attentive and precise in your technique. And not touching your guitar all week, then sitting down on a Saturday night aiming to learn every single barre-chord position from scratch in a five-hour marathon, will give you a serious case of cramped and confused hands—and probably squelch your enthusiasm for playing for a good while.

So how should you approach practicing then? As mentioned elsewhere in these pages, by taking small, well-planned steps. "Just like everything else in your life that you've learned, from the alphabet on, repetition is how you learn," says Cathy Fink. "You have to get comfortable with the concept that you are going to play the same thing 400 times before it comes to you without thinking, and once it comes to you without thinking, you're ready to move on to the next thing.

"What I like to do is to break things down into small steps and say, OK, the first thing you're going to do is practice this technique with your right hand—do that for about five minutes or until it's comfortable. If you start getting hand cramps, stretch out, take a break, shake your fingers around, and come back to it. And then when that feels comfortable, practice your right hand with this one chord under your left hand. Just practice taking off your hand and putting it back on that chord. Breaking things down into those small bits and doing them in the correct sequence really helps people make progress."

When practicing, try to spend at least 15 minutes concentrating on something you need to work on.

The other key to success is practicing regularly—make time every day or close to it, even if you can spare only 20 minutes. "People who practice only once or twice a week will never get any better," says Old Town School of Folk Music guitar teacher Jacob Sweet. "They will only stay in the same spot or regress. It is amazing to me how many of my adult students don't realize this." Short, frequent sessions can be very effective—in fact, 20 minutes of focused practice will pay off more than an hour of distracted, aimless playing.

The way you structure an individual practice session also makes a difference. Give yourself a few minutes to warm up and get in the groove by playing something you can do well and enjoy, rather than diving right into the hard stuff. But don't just coast through the entire session. "Try to spend at least 15 minutes concentrating on something new or something that you know you need to work on," advises Jacob Sweet. "More time is better, of course, but that gets pretty draining for beginners."

You may find a few tools to be useful. Bill Purse finds that practice journals help some people focus on specific goals. "Write yourself a little list," he says. "Where do I want to be with the guitar in six months? Where do I want to be in a year? And then work back from that." Other practice tools include a metronome, for keeping a steady beat as well as disciplining yourself to slow things down and then bring them gradually up to tempo; and a tape or digital recorder, for preserving your lessons and getting honest feedback on what you sound like. If you are working out of books, a music stand makes life much easier—it improves your playing position (no more hunching over the table) as well as your sightlines.

Of course, in this hyper-scheduled age, finding the *time* to play is the greatest challenge for most people—especially adults but increasingly kids as well. As with exercising or brushing your teeth, you need to have a regular time and place for the guitar in order to make it part of your daily life. Find a quiet spot where you won't be interrupted by family members or phone calls, and when the allotted time comes, just go do it before you have a chance to think about all the other stuff you really *should* be doing. If you don't clear the time and defend it, something else will fill the space—this is a law of physics of contemporary life.

If you have a guitar teacher, talk with him or her openly about these time issues—it will be frustrating to both of you if your practicing is not keeping pace with your lessons. Once you agree on a time commitment, your teacher can help you create an effective and realistic practice routine that's cued to the material you're covering in class. A good teacher will be able to map out the sequential steps of learning, rather than throw a whole bunch of new things at you at once, leaving you unsure of where to start.

Many of these things will fall into place very naturally if you just have good music to practice in the first place—songs you really love, coming alive on your guitar note by note. When the excitement is there, the time miraculously becomes available, the goals become clear, and practicing doesn't really feel like practicing at all—it's just *playing.* A period when practicing becomes a real drudge may be an indication that you need to seek out some new inspiration, whether it be a different teacher, an in-store clinic, a jam partner, a good lesson book, or just a CD that lights up your ears and your imagination.

Can I teach myself to play using a method book, or do I really need a teacher?

The first thing to realize is that beginners have learned to play the guitar by every imaginable means—with a teacher, with a book, with a video, from a friend, at a workshop, with a pile of LPs or CDs, or, in older times, from hearing the distant strains of the radio or nothing but a neighbor who plays the banjo. So there is no question of whether you *can* teach yourself with a book—of course you can. The question really is, what are the advantages of in-person instruction vs. using some kind of method?

There is a lot to be said for having at least a few lessons with a teacher at the outset. Fundamental things like good body and hand position are much easier to explain and demonstrate in person, and you don't want to develop bad habits that are hard to break later on. The words in the method book and the notes on the accompanying CD will always be the same, while a good teacher customizes the lessons and repertoire for you. "People make sense of things relating to the guitar in their own special and sometimes convoluted ways," says Jacob Sweet, "and a teacher can adapt the presentation according to that. I have seen no books that are able to do this." You can jam with your teacher, and it can be exciting and illuminating to be that close to a skilled player.

Some teachers rely heavily on published music, while others use their own handouts or no written notation at all.

With many teachers, you can bring in a tape of a favorite song and have it roughly transcribed for you on the spot. If you are in a group rather than a private class, you may get less individual attention, but your fellow beginners are a tremendous resource for support and sharing.

Now how about the strengths of a good method book? It is logically laid out, step by step, whereas teachers can be disorganized and scattershot. Most methods are stylistically open-ended, which you may prefer over a teacher who specializes in a particular kind of music. Everything is presented for you in a nice, neat package, which you can work through at your own pace and come back to as often as you like, even months or years later. By comparison, your scribbled notes from class and your teacher's occasional handouts might not provide very good documentation of what you are learning. Plus, you can loop the same track on an instructional CD 50 times if you want to, while it would drive any teacher bonkers to demonstrate something for you that many times.

Your choice doesn't have to boil down to either a teacher or a book/CD, of course. Some teachers have developed very coherent handouts that give you all the material for easy reference. Some use published methods as well, which can give you the best of both approaches—your teacher can augment the "Red River Valley" type of repertoire in traditional methods with contemporary songs, for instance. And you can record your lessons; a digital recorder like a minidisc is a vast improvement over the cassette for this purpose, as it gives you clean audio that you can edit and then access as quickly as a CD track.

The type of teacher or method that might (or might not) work for you is a very individual matter. Most people wind up trying a variety of approaches over their playing lives—they might start off with a teacher, work with lesson books or songbooks for a while, then go for a period with no formal instruction at all, then sign up for a few workshops when progress seems to be coming to a halt. . . . Your needs will change over time, as will your options, depending on factors like free time, budget, location, and transportation (got wheels?).

What factors should I consider in choosing a teacher?

The place to begin any search for a teacher is with yourself: the better you understand what and who it is you are looking for, the better equipped you will be to make the right choice. What styles of music interest you? What are your goals—to accompany yourself, sing with your family, play instrumental music, join a band, follow along at a jam session? What kind of commitment of time and energy are you ready to make to the guitar? As a beginner, you might not have the answers to all these questions— you might have a burning desire to play but not be sure exactly *what* you want to play. That's fine—the answer will emerge over time. But think about why you are learning the guitar and what you already know about your own tendencies as a student before you meet prospective teachers.

Guitar teachers come to this trade from all sorts of angles and with all sorts of philosophies. Outside of genres like classical guitar, there is nothing even close to a standardized approach, and many/most teachers have no formal training—they have developed their lesson plans on the fly. Teaching provides one of the few sources

of steady income for full-time musicians, so the people giving lessons down at your local shop may be doing so more out of gotta-pay-the-bills necessity than a particular calling to be a teacher. That's OK, as long as they don't feel bitter about not being rock stars and believe that teaching is below them. They should relate well to students, be patient and enthusiastic, and have a clear, well-organized approach. And if they are going to teach you as a beginner, they should like working with beginners. Some teachers really want only advanced students and will be bored going over the basics—and so will you if you take lessons with them.

Teachers should be patient and understanding and have a clear, well-organized approach.

Although it might be tempting to study with the local guitar hero, remember that the best performer may not be the best teacher, and the greatest teacher may not be the greatest performer. Pay more attention to expertise in the classroom than on stage.

Here are some other issues to consider and discuss with prospective teachers. You should be able to locate candidates through music schools, college music departments, and guitar stores and by talking to local players—word usually spreads quickly about good teachers.

Chemistry and communication. Simply put, you have to feel comfortable with your teacher, whether playing, talking, or asking questions—especially questions you think are dumb or overly obvious.

Group vs. private. There are advantages both ways. In a private lesson, obviously the focus is on you and your individual progress. You can ask lots of questions and make specific requests. Your teacher can troubleshoot your technique very effectively. All these things will be harder in a group situation, but on the other hand a group class puts you in touch with others to share tips, commiserate about sore fingers, and maybe even find a picking pal.

"So much of learning an instrument is an isolated process," says Jimmy Tomasello. "It makes all the difference in the world to share and play with others. You learn so much by watching, too. It's like if you want to learn French, you can sit at home with the tapes and books and that's cool; however, get your butt to Paris or Quebec for a week and you're warp-speeding. I always recommend that beginners learn in a group because it's fun to share that initial awkwardness with others instead of one-on-one with a teacher, which could be intimidating to some folks."

Specialties. Find out about any specialties, in style or approach, a teacher has. If the specialties don't match up with your goals, can he or she deliver what it is you are looking for? It's unrealistic, for example, to expect a folkie guitarist to be able to teach you how to shred along with your favorite hard-rock CDs. As a beginner, you may be better off with a teacher who can expose you to a variety of styles that you can choose to pursue later on.

Written music. Some teachers use none, some a little, some a lot. And the notation that they use might be chord diagrams, tablature, standard notation, or some combination of these (see the music notation question below). It's worth asking what they use and why; the answer will clue you into whether their general approach is more by ear or more formal.

Finances. Obviously, you need to know what the lessons cost and whether you can afford them for the longer term. Also find out about policies for scheduling and cancellation. Being a private guitar teacher can be a tough business, so respect your teacher's need for steady and reliable payments from students.

Time commitment. As mentioned above, you should be sure that you will be able to put in the practice time that your teacher expects. You'll find some teachers willing to work with you very casually, others who require a high level of commitment and intensity.

You can do an initial screening of teachers in a conversation, but once you have narrowed down to a likely candidate, take a trial lesson and see how it goes. A good teacher, says Bill Purse, "is kind of a coach and a cheerleader all in one." The playing is ultimately up to you, but there's nothing like having expertise and support on the sidelines.

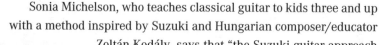

What are some of the essential elements of the Suzuki guitar approach?

The **Suzuki method** is most often associated with classical violin and piano—images of pint-size players ripping through Bach and Vivaldi come to mind. But there are also teachers applying the approach effectively to the guitar, as well as a series of books and tapes that present the lessons and repertoire. Regardless of the instrument, the Suzuki method, developed by the late Japanese violinist and educator Shinichi Suzuki, stems from the belief that kids can learn to play music just as they learned to talk: through listening, repetition, parental involvement, and social interaction. Just as we speak and understand language before we start to read, young Suzuki students develop their ears and basic instrumental technique before turning to the written page.

Sonia Michelson, who teaches classical guitar to kids three and up with a method inspired by Suzuki and Hungarian composer/educator Zoltán Kodály, says that "the Suzuki guitar approach emphasizes the importance of the student-teacher-parent relationship. All three are important for success. Both the teacher and the parent at home need to show kindness, love of music, patience, and encouragement to the young student in order to ensure musical understanding and accomplishment. Dr. Suzuki also stressed the great importance of listening to fine recordings of the best music as being essential to a student's understanding of good tone, phrasing, and musicianship."

Classical guitar teacher Sonia Michelson and students.

Also central to this approach is simply having a good time—Michelson's classes involve lots of rhythm games and other sorts of educational play. This is an axiom that holds no matter what learning method you choose: Have fun, will travel.

Should guitarists learn some type of music notation? If so, what kind?

This is one of those hot-button issues endlessly debated by musicians and teachers. It's actually a more complex question than just "to read or not to read," because guitarists use and swear by several mongrel forms of notation, rather than one standard. As a group, guitarists have a well-deserved rap as bad music readers compared to other instrumentalists, as jazz musicians in particular love to point out. (Sample jab: How do you stop a guitarist from playing? Give him something to read.) But this doesn't change the fact that there is no direct correlation between being a great reader and being a great musician. Music notation is an extremely useful tool but not an end in itself.

Let's sort through this tangle by looking at the pros and cons of the basic types of guitar notation.

CHORD GRIDS

Chord grids (also known as **chord diagrams** or **chord frames**) are the simplest form of guitar-specific notation, understandable to beginners in a matter of minutes. Take a look at these examples.

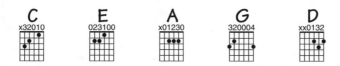

These are visual representations of the guitar fingerboard: The six strings are shown as vertical lines, with the sixth (lowest-pitched) string on the left and the first (highest-pitched) on the right. The dots show where you press down the string, and the numbers up top tell you which finger to use: 1 for the index, 2 for the middle, 3 the ring, 4 the pinky, and sometimes *T* for the thumb. *X* indicates a string that is muted or not played; 0 is an open string. The nut (which guides the strings at the tuner end of the fingerboard) is the thick horizontal line at the top. When the chord is played farther up the neck (toward the soundhole), a Roman numeral to the right of the diagram shows you the **position** (fret).

Closely related to these graphic diagrams is the sort of text-only chord notation you'll see on the Internet, in which the numbers represent the frets and you are left on your own to figure out which finger to put where. For example, an E chord is 022100: open sixth string, second fret on the fifth string, second fret on the fourth string, first fret on the third string, top two strings open. An open D chord would be written XX0232.

The advantages of chord grids? They are clear, visual, and intuitive—very good for showing the basic chords of an accompaniment part. The main disadvantage is that they really work only for chord positions; they can't show you melodies or even little chord riffs. And they also tell you nothing about what notes you are playing, only the location of your fingers.

TABLATURE

Tablature (aka **tab**) is a very old form of notation that has come back with a vengeance and become the dominant way that nonclassical guitarists read music. Also graphically based, tab shows the six strings of the guitar as horizontal lines, with the first string on top and the sixth on the bottom. The numbers indicate which fret you play on a given string.

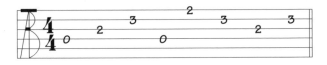

In tab, these lines are divided into measures, as with standard notation, but usually this is the only indication of rhythm that you get—mostly you just follow a sequence of fret positions and have to figure out the rhythm by listening to a recording. Sometimes you will encounter tab that includes rhythmic notation like this:

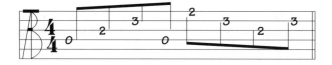

But even here, you are not being shown how long notes ring out—only when they start. This is why tab is commonly used in conjunction with standard notation, which provides the missing information.

"Tab is easy to learn and very specific in the location of notes," says Frederick Noad. "Its weakness is that it does not express time values and sustained parts nearly as well as standard notation. It is worth learning anyway, since it was the original notation for guitar and lute and can be mastered in an hour or two."

Like chord diagrams, tablature shows you where to put your fingers but not what the music should sound like. This makes it a quick but limited way into learning a piece of music. You can play the same notes at several locations on the guitar, so ultimately it's best to see beyond the fret numbers in tablature and be able to hear the notes and perhaps come up with your own interpretation.

Tablature works better for fingerstyle guitar music or flatpicked solos, with their individually articulated notes, than for strumming. Most people also find it indispensable for alternate tunings; when the pitches of open strings are changed, trying to figure out a piece from standard notation only can cause cerebral meltdown.

STANDARD NOTATION

Standard notation is what works for most other instruments—it tells you the pitch, rhythm, and duration of notes all in one compact package. Guitar music written this way often includes fingering information: little numbers next to noteheads tell you which fretting finger to use, and letters tell you which picking finger to use: *p* for thumb, *i* for index, *m* for middle, *a* for ring, *c* for pinky. Circled numbers indicate on which string to play a note, and often other interpretive guidance is given as well.

Among guitarists, you will most often find standard notation readers in the classical realm. Although "classics in tab" editions have become more common, the bulk of the repertoire is written only in standard notation. For classical players, says Ben Harbert, "in the long run, reading music is essential. Understanding phrasing, reading dynamics, having flexibility in fingerings, and transposing music from other instruments are all important parts of being a classical guitarist. I believe that students who have some experience with the guitar can begin with tab; otherwise, learning to read music can slow a student enough to be frustrated with the style. But the students I begin on tab inevitably want to learn to read music after they see the limitations of tab. And students with no experience can learn to read music at the level of their technical progress on the guitar."

The main advantage of standard notation, as alluded to above, is that it represents the actual sound of the notes rather than simply where you put your fingers, so it encourages you to listen more closely and make your own interpretation. It shows you the contour of a melody very clearly and includes a lot of detail about the feel, dynamics, and other nuances of the music. As for disadvantages, the primary one is that standard notation is simply harder to learn than tab or chord diagrams—although not nearly as hard as most guitarists think. It is more suited to solo instrumentals than to simple accompaniments, which are very efficiently shown with chord diagrams or tab, and it is inadequate for alternate-tunings styles.

NO NOTATION

From blues to flamenco, plenty of genres have flourished without a written note in sight. In the case of flamenco, as Frederick Noad points out, "a good ear and skill at memorizing are of the first importance. In Spain there was a time when guitarists who could read music were excluded from the flamenco fraternity." With the boom of instructional publishing, just about every style—including flamenco—is available transcribed and notated these days, but you can still make a lifetime of music without cracking open a single piece of sheet music.

In the end, keep in mind that music notation of whatever form is just shorthand. It allows someone else to communicate a piece of music to you on paper, or for you to jot down an idea for safekeeping or to share with other musicians. The further you go as a player, the more likely it is that you will want or need to do these things. There are limitations to what you can do as a musician—especially as a professional musician—without learning the written language.

But no matter what sort of notation you wind up using or not using, the essential thing is to be able to *hear* the music coming out of your guitar, rather than remain focused on fret numbers or chord shapes or eighth notes or anything else on the page.

Do you recommend using videos for learning?

Some people are visual learners, and seeing and hearing a guitarist/teacher on the TV screen illuminates things for them better than a whole stack of books. There is an incredible array of material available on video these days, from beginner instruction through demonstrations of signature songs by famous guitarists of every stripe. The production values are generally excellent, with crisp audio, professional lighting, and split-screen close-ups of both hands on the guitar. Tab booklets are usually included as well. For those interested in artists who predate the instructional-video age, there are also performance videos available giving extraordinary views of the legends of jazz, blues, country, rock, and other genres in concert and in early broadcasts.

For all these reasons, videos have become popular parts of the guitar library. But they have some weaknesses, too. They are (at this

point, anyway) cumbersome if you want to find a specific song or passage; the old-fashioned book and the newfangled CD are much better for quick access than the rewind button on the VCR. Videos are also expensive to make and expensive to buy—you could probably pick up two or three CD lesson books for the price of one artist

There is an incredible array of material available on video these days.

video, and a single book usually includes significantly more material than a single video.

From my perspective, videos are a great supplement to other ways of learning. They are the closest you will probably come to getting a private lesson with a guitar hero, and they can reveal secrets that you would never be able to see by craning your neck at a concert. You should realize, however, that many videos (especially those by big stars who rarely teach) deliver more of an intimate performance than an actual "lesson."

What kind of guitar instruction is available on the computer? How does this medium compare with books and videos?

Like all things digital, computer-based guitar instruction is evolving at a dizzying pace. The state-of-the-art programs as I began writing this answer will probably be obsolete by the end of the last paragraph, so I won't even try to pin down precisely what you can do with your guitar and your PC.

The potential is tremendous, though. Web sites, CD-ROMs, DVDs, and the like can deliver a dazzling combination of audio, video, music notation, text, and interactive features that no other medium can match. You can click your way to the exact video view or piece of information you want, watch the lyrics and tab scroll by, and slow down the music while maintaining the same pitch. You can plug in your guitar and see on screen how well you are following along, or jam along with a virtual backup band. Software will help you look up a zillion chords in whatever tuning you like, zip through an encyclopedia of scales and modes, or simply tune your guitar.

The gee-whiz factor with computer instruction is very high; the challenge, as always, is for developers to bring solid teaching approaches to bear on the latest and hottest technology. Especially as a beginner, what you need is not unlimited options or techno razzle-dazzle but a smartly sequenced, clearly presented progression of lessons.

The pace of change in the computer world is both its greatest strength and its greatest weakness. You know how quickly that cutting-edge computer/software/peripheral winds up in a dusty box in your basement. Computer-based instruction on a fixed medium like CD-ROM or DVD can be expected to have a similarly short shelf life—it's entirely possible that eventually you won't even be able to open that disc on your PC, because the engine that runs it has disappeared from the market, and you had to replace the machine that did run it with something that keeps pace with the industry's latest offerings. And even if the disc still runs, it will quickly seem extremely primitive and limited compared to what's come out since. So don't expect any program to be useful as long as more stable media like books or even CDs and videos will be. But if you get a lot of value from it in the short term, great—grab your guitar and your mouse and have a blast.

These days, the Web and a high-speed connection to it are your best ticket to checking out what's available in multimedia guitar instruction. Free lessons, freeware, and shareware abound, and there are massive libraries of song lyrics and guitar tab. It's easy to find fellow computer/guitar heads who can recommend programs and sites as well as offer playing tips. Over time, expect to see more and more personalized instruction available on the Web, private as well as small group lessons with students scattered all over the globe. Where all

The Web and a high-speed connection to it are your best ticket to checking out what's available in multimedia guitar instruction.

this technology is going is never clear, but this much is definitely true: your computer can open up new horizons for you as a guitarist.

Are there any secrets to figuring out songs by ear?

The more you play and the more you listen, the sharper you will be at recognizing patterns and chord shapes in songs that you hear. After a while, the distinctive sound of an open G chord becomes ingrained in your memory, and when you hear a guitarist kicking off a song with that chord, you'll know it—bingo. The same holds true for all sorts of chords and licks: they eventually become part of a vocabulary of sounds that you recognize without even thinking.

There are some tips and tools that can help you along the way. Before you can get anywhere in figuring out a song, you need to be sure that you are in tune with the record. This is often a simple matter of tuning your guitar with an electronic tuner, but that doesn't work if the record isn't exactly at normal pitch—especially with older recordings, you may have to tweak your tuning slightly up or down.

The first thing I do is listen for what's called the **tonic**: the root note of the key that the song is in. For a song in the key of G, the tonic is a G note; in the key of C, it's a C; and so on. The tonic is the harmonic center of the song—the chords may travel away from that note, but eventually they come back and resolve on it. To find this note, first try your open sixth (E), fifth (A), fourth (D), and third (G) strings and see if any of them match the song you are trying to work out—E, A, D, and G are all very common keys for guitar songs. If those don't fit, play notes up and down the sixth string while listening to the track; you will feel it when you arrive at that critical note. If the note you are playing sounds very close to, but not precisely on, the tonic, and moving up or down a fret takes you further away, that's a clue that you may need to retune slightly.

Once you've got that note, you need to know what sort of chord sits on it. Let's say the tonic is a D—is it a bright-sounding D major or a darker, moodier D minor? Your ears will learn to tell the difference. I would recommend first trying out this process on simple folk, country, or rock songs with just a few chords, and the tonic chord will almost always be a simple major or minor chord.

From here, learning a little bit about the chords typically found in each key is extremely helpful. I won't get into full-on description of chord theory here, and your eyes may be glazing over at the very mention of the *t* word. Suffice it to say that a little dab of chord theory goes a long way in picking up music by ear. Here is a chart that shows the basic chords in the most common guitar keys (for simplicity's sake, I have left out some of the more complicated and less common chords). The Roman numerals in the top row indicate which degree of the scale the chord is built on (uppercase Roman numerals are used for major chords, and lowercase for minor). The I is the tonic chord, which tells you what key you're in (e.g., G is the I chord in the key of G; G is the first note of the scale in that key). The next most common chords are the IV and V (built on the fourth and fifth notes in the scale), and the other chords in the same row are likely suspects too. So if you have found that the song is in the key of A, for instance, look across the A row for other chords that are likely to crop up in your song, especially the IV (D) and V (E).

Major Keys

I	ii	iii	IV	V or V7	vi
C	Dm	Em	F	G or G7	Am
D	Em	F#m	G	A or A7	Bm
E	F#m	G#m	A	B or B7	C#m
G	Am	Bm	C	D or D7	Em
A	Bm	C#m	D	E or E7	F#m

Minor Keys

i	III	iv	v or V7	VI	VII or VII7
Am	C	Dm	Em or E7	F	G or G7
Em	G	Am	Bm or B7	C	D or D7
Dm	F	Gm	Am or A7	Bb	C or C7

Also very useful is some understanding of common **chord progressions**: sequences of chords that crop up again and again in songs. If you know, for instance, that the V chord usually resolves to the I chord, you have a significant clue to where the chord progression might go in your song. You know this intuitively—when you're playing or listening to something in the key of C, for instance, you feel the tug from a G chord (the V) back toward C (the I). But knowing this fact intellectually as well as intuitively is another arrow in your quiver.

In addition to using this kind of information to help you find the chords, you can apply the method mentioned above of searching for the root of a particular chord by trying open strings or moving around the sixth string. Once you know the root, it's pretty easy to zero in on the exact chord.

As you spin the song, listen closely for open strings, which have a bright ring that's distinctly different from fretted notes. Most guitarists use chords with a lot of open strings—call it laziness, or call it just being smart. This brings up one very important rule for learning songs off records: the correct answer is most likely the easiest one. If you find yourself having to tie your fingers into knots to play along, you are probably missing some essential piece of information.

Like the presence of a capo. Let's say you've discovered that a song by your favorite songwriter/guitarist is in the knuckle-busting key of E♭. But you could swear that you hear something that sounds like a D chord, with maybe an A and G thrown in there too. What's going on here? Most likely, a capo at the first fret, which raises those D, A, and G fingerings so that you hear them as E♭, B♭, and A♭. Aha! Take a look at the capo question in the Essential Accessories chapter for more information on how these little gizmos work to make difficult keys easy to play in.

A bigger monkey wrench is thrown in when the song is not played in standard tuning—you will hear open strings ringing that are simply not available on your guitar. Identifying alternate tunings by ear can be tough, which is why many people rely on transcriptions in magazines and songbooks and on the Web to supply the critical information about how the guitar is tuned. Artist sites often include lists of tunings that are invaluable. If the tuning or transcription was posted by a fan on an "unofficial" site, it may or may not be correct, but even checking out an inaccurate version may give you ideas about how to do it right. And coming up with your own rendition, in a different tuning or even in standard tuning, is just as valid as re-creating the original.

Even if the song is not in a weird tuning, these in-print or on-line transcriptions are a great resource. A few decades ago, all songbooks were oriented toward piano players, and the guitar chords shown were totally unrealistic—they showed me, for instance, that James Taylor had a particular fondness for E♭ and B♭ chords, when in reality he was often just playing D and A chords and using a capo. Nowadays, many guitar songbooks and published transcriptions are anatomically correct, with tunings and capo positions and all.

In the heyday of the LP, lots of musicians learned songs by slowing the album down to half speed, which was a great trick but had the unfortunate side effect of lowering all the notes by an octave. These days there are stand-alone boxes and software that do the same thing without changing the pitch—very handy "hearing aids" used by professional transcribers all the time.

So there are plenty of tools potentially at your disposal, but remember that going through this process with nothing but your ears and your fingers is educational way beyond figuring out how to play a specific song. You learn a tremendous amount by trying to pin down how to re-create sounds without following a written recipe. Even if you get it wrong, through trial and error you discover a lot about how songs and guitars work. And hey, more than a few great songs were written this way: trying and failing to figure out how to play one song, you stumble on something else that sounds cool. And that is more valuable than any note-perfect version of someone else's song would ever be.

Alternate tunings are simply what you get when you twiddle the notes of your open strings away from the pitches E A D G B E (from the lowest-pitched string to the highest), also known as standard tuning.

What are alternate tunings, and why do so many guitarists use them?

This is not a new idea. Standard tuning came into being around the late 1700s, and the guitar family goes back a lot further than that. The concept of tuning the strings to a chord (often called an **open tuning**) is basic to blues and other traditions. Modern guitarists may feel that they are on the cutting edge by using different tunings for different songs, but they are simply the latest in a long line of stringed-instrument players to do this.

The simplest alternate tuning, and the one that just about everybody uses, is known as **dropped D**: lowering the sixth string to D. When you also drop the first string to D, you've got **double dropped D** (aka **D modal**), widely used by Neil Young and others. The most common open tunings are **open G** (D G D G B D, a G-major chord), **open D** (D A D F♯ A D, a D-major chord), and **open C** (C G C G C E, a C-major chord). Open G and open D are the staples of slide guitar and country blues. Also popular in Celtic music and other genres is the tuning referred to as **"dad gad"**: D A D G A D. From there, the variations are endless.

So why bother changing the tuning of your guitar and thereby hopelessly confusing your hard-earned knowledge of where notes are on the fingerboard? First, to make things easier by making certain notes available on open strings. If you are playing a song in the key of D, dropped-D tuning is very convenient because it gives you a nice low root note on the sixth string. If you are playing slide, having the open strings tuned to a chord means that you can play melodies and licks over the open strings—simultaneous lead and backup—and then play other big fat chords by moving your slide up the neck. Tunings can make chord fingerings very simple; Jessica Baron Turner starts kids in open-G tuning because it allows them to play a G chord with no fretting fingers and then versions of the D and C chords with only two fingers.

In an alternate tuning, you can also play complex chords with very little effort—a Dm7(add6) is actually accomplished with just two fingers once you are in double-dropped-D tuning. In fact, with an alternate tuning, you can play chord voicings that are unreachable in standard tuning. For songwriters and instrumentalists looking for new sounds, this is a major attraction—play impossible jazz chords without even trying! And the kicker is that you don't have to know what you're doing, theoretically speaking: if you are in an unfamiliar tuning, what you know about fingerings no longer applies, so you can freely hunt and peck and experiment. You can even play chords and licks you know in standard tuning and hear what bizarre sounds come out! Alternate-tunings junkies talk about this process in mystical tones—they love getting lost in an entirely new guitar landscape and discovering sounds they never would have found intentionally or consciously. As Joni Mitchell once put it, changing your tuning is like rearranging the letters on your keyboard and then typing away—you are sure to come up with some new words!

Sounds enticing, doesn't it? It is, but alternate tunings can also be very confusing, especially if you are just gaining your footing (finger-ing, I mean) on the guitar. So as a beginner, you should stick to one tuning until you've gained some experience. Standard tuning is plen-ty to keep anyone busy, and it has its own unique advantages, such as the flexibility to give you open-string roots in a variety of keys. It is good to realize, though, that a whole new universe of sounds becomes available by retuning your strings, and in many styles of contempo-rary music, alternate tunings are challenging the very "standardness" of standard tuning.

We Homo sapiens love to measure our achievements with numbers: I make $50,000, I can jog seven miles, my song is No. 1 on the charts. But playing music—as

How long will it take me to get good at the guitar?

opposed to selling music—can't be quantified like this. And what exact-ly does it mean to be good/better/best at the guitar? Is the jazz player who knows lots of fancy moves but sounds just like everyone else a bet-ter player than the guy who sings powerful, poetic songs but only knows ten chords? Is someone good if she's on a cloud because she just got down her first real solo guitar piece? How about the experienced player who has a large repertoire but feels like he's in a slump and just rehashing the same old stuff? The value of music lies in the intangible pleasures it brings to the player and the listener, not in the ka-ching of product sales or in some athletic measure of techni-cal ability.

The point is that there is no easy answer to the question of how much time will pass until you feel you have arrived at a level of com-petence on the guitar. Nor should there be an easy answer. As a begin-ner, you are eager to get to a point where things start falling into place—this is what drives you to grin and bear those sore fingers, keep wrestling with that barre chord, and practice that lick over and over. And sooner or later, all those awkward moves will become sec-ond nature and then connect into a stream of what is undeniably *music*. But the feeling of not quite being where you want to be never goes away: no matter how much you learn, there's always a horizon of things you haven't learned. In fact, the more you advance, the more aware you become of the musical possibilities just beyond your reach. The ceaseless pursuit of those possibilities is what makes great musicians great.

Even so, down in the trenches of learning, we all need ways to measure and acknowledge our day-to-day progress. This is why, as discussed in the practicing section above, teachers recommend setting small, achievable goals that you can check off the list with the satisfying knowledge that you couldn't do it before and now you can. And then onto the next thing . . .

In my mind, the ultimate measure of progress is the pleasure you get out of playing. If you're fired up to crack open that case all the time, I'd say you're progressing nicely, regardless of what technical hurdles you might or might not have overcome. You're inspired because you are making music, and in my book, that means you're *good.*

SHARING YOUR MUSIC

As a private creative outlet, there's nothing better than playing music—the partnership of you and your guitar can bring deep emotional and spiritual fulfillment. This experience is all some people want from music, and if

I'm too shy to play guitar in front of anyone but my dog. How can I break the ice?

you fit that description, there's no need to feel as if you have to force yourself into making some big public statement—your bedroom is no less valid a venue than a concert hall.

On the other hand, there's an extraordinary power in music as a social activity, played for or with friends, family, or strangers, and often the only things keeping people from discovering it are their insecurities or shyness. That certainly was the case—and is the case—for me. I've been lucky enough to encounter other people who egged me into doing what I secretly wanted to do but could never get up the nerve to initiate. In high school, a fellow guitarist with similar tastes in music but a totally different personality—a reckless extrovert—decided that I was going to be his picking partner, regardless of what I thought about the idea. Thank God for his stubbornness, because it led me eventually to regular performances, a songwriting collaboration, and a band that transformed my entire experience of high school and then college. The guy sure knew how to break the ice!

There are all kinds of things you can do to start sharing music with others. One of the easiest ways to connect with other beginners is through a group class, workshop, or music camp. Or you can just try networking. The world is full of people in the same boat as you, and getting together with them does more than just break through your isolation. Carol McComb, who has been teaching beginner classes for decades, says that in a group lesson, "there is something

Connecting with other beginning guitarists can turbo-charge your learning.

about the social part, or the community part, of playing music together. . . . I just think people learn faster—they learn incredibly fast. I can teach my students in ten weeks what I learned in a year on my own. That's amazing. They are looking around the room and seeing all these other people, and they share information— 'Ooh, I went to this concert,' or, 'I broke a string last night and I tried to put one on, and it felt so good when I got it.' And they sing together—it's just neat.

"I also teach at music camps," she adds, "and there is a built-in way for people to jam together. I would say that probably almost every student I've ever had who has gotten together with another musician to play has found it more fun than playing on her own. Not too many enjoy playing alone more than playing with others."

A jam partner doesn't have to be a beginner, either. You may think you're not good enough to satisfy a more skilled player, but you both can gain a lot from the experience—a lead guitarist might like nothing better than to have a rhythm player to practice with, for instance. "If you really want to learn stuff," advises Cathy Fink, "get together with someone who just learned what you want to learn. They are not so far advanced that it's below them to show you, and usually they are so excited that they just learned something that they love the idea that somebody else wants to find out how to do it. We see this happening at music camps all the time. Sometimes we'll specifically pair up one of our beginners with one of our intermediate players, so they can learn a little bit from each other. The intermediate player learns something from the process of slowing down what they just learned how to play, and the beginner has somebody a little bit ahead to give him some encouragement."

Jam sessions and group classes have the side benefit of getting you a little more comfortable with the idea of getting up and playing for people by yourself. This step is often scary but incredibly rewarding; sharing your music with someone is a great and rare gift, no matter how limited you feel your abilities are. Just think small: say to a family member or confidant, "Hey, want to hear this song I've been working on?" Give it a shot, and don't apologize for flubs or whatever you can't do—try to see the glass as half full. If the solo spotlight is too bright, look for opportunities to accompany a sing-along, maybe alongside another instrumentalist. The holidays are an ideal time to do this, and your effort will be much appreciated.

Your shyness may never go away entirely—it surely hasn't for me, and many seasoned performers still get those same butterflies. But the more frequently you air your music in public, the easier it gets. It's irrelevant whether you have the desire to do anything remotely "professional" with music, now or down the road. Music wants to be shared, and doing so will spark new friendships, deepen old ones, and turbocharge your playing. Paul Kotapish, a multi-instrumentalist and one of the most voracious jammers I've ever had the pleasure to know, boils down his advice to beginners to this: "Learn a chord, and start a band." Or here's a modified version for those with more cautious personalities: Learn a chord, and show someone how nice it sounds.

How can I find people to jam with, and how should I prepare for those sessions?

Jam sessions come in all shapes and sizes, from siblings belting out pop hits to campfire song circles to house parties to sit-ins down at the jazz club or Irish pub. Although some of these confabs have an element of competitiveness, good jams are all about good times and companionship, and a beginner strumming along is as welcome as a professional guitar slinger.

It can be hard to find or start a jam session, but once one gets going, it is even harder to stop. Prime places to scout for jam sessions or playing partners have been mentioned elsewhere in these pages: guitar classes, music camps, festivals, music stores . . . A guitar shop might have a board where you can post a notice about your interests and ability level and who/what you are looking for. Local publications, especially free ones, sometimes have active "musicians' exchange" listings, and many Web sites also feature musician classifieds and referral services, although they cast a very wide geographical net. Open-mic nights draw players of all stripes and can be a great place for making connections, even if you are not taking the stage. In many communities there are small organizations of musicians and aficionados—for songwriters, folkies, blues mavens, etc. Poke and ask around; you might be surprised at what you find in your town.

In a jam session, rhythm rules. Concentrate on nailing the chord changes and keeping a steady beat.

When you do meet someone, it is a big help if you can concretely describe your interests beyond "I listen to all kinds of stuff," even if that is the case. Make a short list of artists and records you love. And start collecting songs you play or want to play in a notebook: think especially about songs that others might know, are straightforward to pick or sing along with, and are more on the festive side than moody personal reflections. Jam sessions often have awkward moments when everyone is rifling through their internal song indexes to think of the next thing to play, and your songbook could really keep things moving. And if you can come up with that fourth verse that eludes everyone else's memory, you are a major asset to the group! Also, there are some great books available for finding lyrics and song ideas (one I find particularly useful is *Rise Up Singing*—see the Resources chapter).

Aside from your songbook, a capo is a very handy jam-session accessory in many situations. It allows you to change the key to suit people's voices or instruments better, without having to play different fingerings. If another guitarist slaps on a capo at the second fret and starts playing something, match that capo position and watch his or her fingers—that'll make it much easier to join in.

Effective jam session preparations will vary depending on the style and setting, but there are a few universal truths. Most important, rhythm rules, so work hard on nailing the chord changes and keeping a steady beat. Simplify a part you are still trying to master down to something that you can do without thinking or pausing. Without solid rhythm, everything falls apart, whereas the frills can go away and not be missed at all. Also, train yourself to listen and be flexible with the arrangement of a song—you might need to let an intro chord sit there for a few extra measures, for instance, while the singer is trying to think of the next verse. When someone is singing or taking a lead, kick back and give them room to be heard. And finally, stick with a winning theme. If everyone is having a blast singing Beatles songs, try to come up with something in the same vein. If you don't know anything along those lines, do a little homework before your next gathering. Everyone will light up when you kick into one of their favorite songs—it's like discovering you have a close friend in common.

Let's see . . . a quick flip through *Acoustic Guitar* magazine's annual guide to summer workshops reveals courses in acoustic blues and slide, chamber music for classical guitar and mandolin, six- and seven-string Brazilian guitar and cavaquinho, Cape Breton fiddle tunes, rock soloing, western swing, songwriting, alternate tunings, music theory, and Gypsy jazz—not to mention building and repairing guitars—in locations from Manhattan to Mallorca. You get the idea. Whether your taste runs to Appalachian ballads or rocking zydeco, you'll probably be able to find a workshop for it.

What kind of camps or workshops are there for guitarists?

But, you may be thinking, aren't camps just for young kids? Well, yes, some music camps are, but others are specifically for high school or college students, and grown-ups have caught on to the fact that they

can have an awfully good time immersing themselves in their favorite music with fellow fanatics. So nowadays there are camps catering to all ages and styles, some following the traditional camp model of a rustic setting with camping or cabins, others taking place in comfortable hotels or at urban locations with day-only attendance. The vibe of these gatherings varies quite a bit, from nonstop revelry to more studious and structured atmospheres.

Music camps and workshops (a National Guitar Workshop classroom is shown here) cater to all ages and musical styles.

Many professional players enjoy taking a hiatus from the road and teaching at these camps, so you will find opportunities to study with people whose music you know and love. And, of course, your fellow campers are a big draw. Jamming tends to happen all over the place and at all hours, and at many camps the instructors help to organize and lead sessions. There are also usually open-mic venues for those who want a taste of the stage.

Most camps offer extensive beginner programs, and you can learn an awful lot in a week of living and breathing guitar music (don't forget to sleep at least a little). Beyond good old word-of-mouth, Web sites offer complete information about camps, so surf around for options that fit your personality, interests, and budget (see the Resources chapter for a few starting points). Find out about what sorts of beginner classes camps offer, and if guided slow jams and other beginner-oriented activities are part of the package.

If you feel that you are pursuing your music in isolation, or that every other guitarist in the world is much more skilled and savvy than you are, a camp is a surefire cure. You will see that everyone has to clear the same basic hurdles in learning an instrument and that music really takes flight when you gather with kindred spirits.

You can gain valuable performing experience without going anywhere near a stage. Start right at your house: a parent, sibling, spouse, or close friend can make a great first audience for a set that could consist of only one song. You might be able to coax someone into singing or playing with you, which can make things more comfortable the first time out. Further afield, look for playing opportunities at parties, barbecues, and other social gatherings. And if you are ready to put together an actual set list and do a little show, you can find extremely appreciative and thoroughly nonintimidating audiences at places like senior centers and schools. Some of my favorite "gigs" have been playing and singing alongside my daughter in preschool and elementary school, where the kids really show you when they like something (and when they are bored!), and where simplicity goes over better than anything tricky. The practice time with my daughter at home has been as rewarding as the show itself.

When you are ready for a more formal performance situation, open-mic nights are a perfect place to get your feet wet on an actual stage with a real PA system, and they have the fringe benefit of introducing you to fellow musicians in the area. You usually are limited to one or two songs, so no extensive repertoire is required, and relative beginners are often part of the lineup. When I moved to the San Francisco Bay Area after college in tandem with my brother, open mics were our introduction to the entire local scene, and one of them led eventually to a regular once-a-month bar gig. Scores of solo artists and bands have gotten started this way. It might seem intimidating to play for an audience of primarily musicians, but they have been exactly in your shoes, and for the most part I have found them to be appreciative and supportive. Even full-time pros use open mics as places to test out new material or just scratch their itch to get on stage, and I have recognized "name" players at open mics on more than one occasion.

Your first song has to allow both you and your audience to get into the groove.

Then there are the casual settings where your audience may or may not pay any attention to you— cafés, restaurants, bookstores, receptions, office parties, the street . . . the bread-and-butter (or bagel-and-cream-cheese) gigs for many musicians. Is it depressing to play guitar for people while they clink their glasses and talk about the traffic and never notice that you just executed a particularly soulful rendition of a classic song? Sure, it can be. But it's also liberating. These sorts of gigs can be like a heightened form of practice, with only one time through each tune (except on the street, where you can play the same five songs all day if you want to) and the possibility of tip money. If a song does break through the chatter and get a reaction, that is a minor miracle and very gratifying.

A well-planned set list is a big advantage in performing. Your first song has to allow both you and your audience to get into the groove, so make it something you can play in a relaxed fashion, and save your tough stuff for later. Think about all the many types of contrasts from song to song, and incorporate changes of key, tempo, length, and mood. These are good both for your audience's ears and for you as a player to stay at the top of your game.

The best way to get ready for a performance of any type is to practice as realistically as you can. That means do a true dress rehearsal: Sit if you are going to sit, stand if you're going to stand, and start at the beginning and go right through to the end without restarting any songs or stopping for ten minutes of tuning and snacking. If you make a mistake, force yourself to plow ahead in the least awkward manner possible. Recovering from flubs is an essential performing skill, and you can practice it. Just keep the rhythm going and circle back around to the beginning of the line, or forget about your mistake and concentrate on nailing the rest of the song—your audience will forget about your momentary lapse, if they even noticed it in the first place.

It's an adrenaline rush to put yourself out there for an audience and feel the energy waves come back at you. You may get hooked and decide to dedicate yourself to doing this for a living. But remember that you can perform music for people without ever becoming a Performer, with a press kit and glossy photo and stage gear. Don't let a lack of career aspirations stop you from experiencing the buzz of sharing your music. Playing guitar is much too important an activity to be left to the professionals.

There is a natural ebb and flow to learning—I don't think it's possible or even desirable to be blasting ahead all the time. You might pick up a whole bunch of new things really fast, then need to spend a period of time assimilating all that information and resting up for the next challenges.

Sometimes I feel like my playing is in a rut, and I start to lose interest. What can I do to stay inspired?

We have so much instant gratification available to us these days, from pay-per-view cable to on-line shopping, that it is easy to become impatient with the pace of learning an instrument. No matter how hard you practice or how good your guitar is or how sophisticated the method you are using, it just takes time to advance. Not only are you developing calluses and training minute muscles in your fingers, but you are constantly refining your internal sense of harmony, melody, and rhythm. Actually practicing the guitar is only part of what helps us improve. The rest of the progress is in the expansion of our soul and imagination, and time spent away from the guitar can do as much to develop these intangible things as concentrated playing.

Still, everybody experiences that feeling of being in a rut, and the accompanying drain of enthusiasm for the guitar. There are many things that might help nudge you back on the road. Maybe you've gone as far as you can with your teacher, book, video, or whatever tool you are using, and some new instruction with a different approach might be just the ticket. If you have been in a group class, maybe some individual attention is what you need, or if you have been taking private lessons, maybe some group interaction would do wonders for you. As elaborated above, connecting with other musicians is a real energizer. Another player will always have somewhat different interests than you do, and trying to find common ground will suggest new projects or goals and give you a powerful incentive to achieve them.

Or you might need to simply open your ears a little wider. Everything we hear is ultimately the fuel for everything we play, and a new artist or style—especially experienced in person rather than on record—might suggest avenues for the guitar that you have never even considered or may simply rekindle the flame that started you on this playing quest in the first place.

It is easy to fall into the trap of blaming your guitar for a lack of progress, and some of the greatest guitar music of all time has been made on cheap instruments that any guitar snob would snort at. But it is possible to reach a point at which your guitar limits what you can do, and a new, better, or just plain different instrument can inspire a new wave of learning. Oftentimes you're not even really aware of the ways in which a particular guitar shapes the music you play on it. For a long time I played a small-bodied instrument that sounded very nice for solo fingerstyle music, which I hadn't explored much at all before. When I replaced it with a bigger instrument that had a much fuller sound and volume to burn, I suddenly rediscovered the raw power of rock rhythm and started playing all kinds of songs in that vein. So if you suspect your current guitar is holding you back somehow, you might try browsing in music stores or borrowing something different— but only do this if you are prepared to follow through on getting a new guitar. No sense in deepening your dissatisfaction with an instrument that you are going to be playing for the foreseeable future—and there is still plenty of undiscovered music in that guitar anyway.

For me, what sparks progress on the guitar is having some kind of project; arbitrarily selecting something (picking exercises or a song out of a book that contains certain technical challenges, for instance) never works—I lack that kind of discipline, I guess. The projects that really stick come organically out of listening, preparing for an upcoming gig or get-together, or exploring a new idea I happen upon. My guitar is never more alive for me than it is when I am writing a song—I will play something over and over till my fingers are killing me, trying to get my head and hands around it and understand where it is leading. The same thing holds true regardless of whether you write songs or "compose" in any formal sense: what drives learning are these moments when you can feel music being created right under your fingers.

Not a bad accomplishment for two hands, some pieces of wood, and six strings.

RESOURCES

The guitar instruction field is teeming with products.   **Instruction**
Here are a few written by people interviewed for this
book or mentioned specifically in the text. For a broad selection,
browse a local music store or one of the catalogs listed under mail-
order sources below.

Peter Blood-Patterson, ed., *Rise Up Singing*, Sing Out. Extremely use-
    ful compendium of lyrics and chord progressions for 1,200 songs.
    Strong folk orientation, but a good sampling of '60s and '70s
    pop/rock as well.
Cathy Fink and Marcy Marxer, *Kids' Guitar Songbook*, Homespun.
    Individually and together, Fink and Marxer have a number of
    other good books and videos. For a complete list, see www.
    cathymarcy.com.
Carol McComb, *Country and Blues Guitar for the Musically Hopeless*,
    Klutz Press.
Sonia Michelson, *New Dimensions in Classical Guitar for Children*, Mel
    Bay. Companion books of classical repertoire for kids are also
    available.
Frederick Noad, *Solo Guitar Playing*, Vols. 1 and 2, Schirmer; *The*

Complete Idiot's Guide to Playing the Guitar, Macmillan.

Jessica Baron Turner, *SmartStart Guitar,* Hal Leonard. A kids' guitar method, in book/CD or on video.

Instruments

Acoustic Guitar Owner's Manual, String Letter Publishing.

Tony Bacon, *Electric Guitars: The Illustrated Encyclopedia,* Thunder Bay.

Dan Erlewine, *Guitar Player Repair Guide: How to Set Up, Maintain, and Repair Electrics and Acoustics,* Backbeat Books.

Frets.com. Frank Ford's exhaustive, authoritative site on acoustic guitar care and repair.

Mail-Order Sources

Elderly Instruments
PO Box 14249
Lansing, MI 48901-4249
(517) 372-7890
Fax (517) 372-5155
www.elderly.com
Comprehensive catalog of guitar books and products, with useful descriptions.

JK Lutherie
11115 Sand Run
Harrison, OH 45030
Orders (800) 344-8880
(513) 353-3320
www.jklutherie.com
Specializes in instrument books.

Music Dispatch
www.musicdispatch.com
(800) 637-2852
Fax (414) 774-3259
Mail-order for Hal Leonard Publishing and its many distributed lines.

P.J. Ballantine
PO Box 10393
Van Nuys, CA 91410
(888) 310-3342
www.pjballantine.com
Music instruction from various publishers.

Sheetmusicdirect.com
Downloadable sheet music.

Sheetmusicplus.com
1322 Pacific Ave.
San Francisco, CA 94109
(800) 480-6041
Fax (415) 931-8819
Extensive catalog from many
publishers.

String Letter Publishing
PO Box 767
San Anselmo, CA 94979-0767
(415) 485-6946
Fax (415) 485-0831
www.stringletter.com
The publisher of this book offers
a variety of guitar instruction
and reference works, including
The Acoustic Guitar Method (fall
2001), with free sample lessons
on the Web site.

The following is a small sampling of organizations
that run workshops and camps. For an extensive,
searchable list, with links and specialties (updated annually), visit
www.acousticguitar.com.

Music Camps

Augusta Heritage Center
Davis and Elkins College
100 Campus Dr.
Elkins, WV 26241
(304) 637-1209
Fax (304) 637-1317
www.augustaheritage.com

Berklee College of Music
1140 Boylston St.
Boston, MA 02215
(617) 266-1400
Fax (617) 747-2047
www.berklee.edu

Centrum
PO Box 1158
Port Townsend, WA 98368-0958
(360) 385-3102
Fax (360) 385-2470
www.centrum.org

National Guitar Workshops
PO Box 222
Lakeside, CT 06758
(800) 234-6479
Fax (860) 567-0374
www.guitarworkshop.com

Suzuki Association of the Americas
PO Box 17310
Boulder, CO 80308
(303) 444-0948
Fax (303) 444-0984
www.suzukiassociation.org

The Swannanoa Gathering
Warren Wilson College
PO Box 9000
Asheville, NC 28815-9000
(828) 298-3434
Fax (828) 299-3326
www.swangathering.org

Other Web Resources

Acoustic Guitar Central, www.acousticguitar.com. The on-line arm of *Acoustic Guitar* magazine offers features, reviews, lessons, and forums (including one specifically for beginners).

Harmony-central.com. Comprehensive musicians' site.

Guitar.com. Tablature, gear info, forums, and more.

Tabcrawler.com. For locating on-line tablature.

Wholenote.com. Free lessons and other services.

INDEX OF GUITAR LINGO

Page numbers indicate where a term is most fully explained and illustrated.

0 33
00 33
000 33
A 440 .66
acoustic guitar 13
action 36
alternate tuning 99
archtop guitar 16
auditorium (body size) 33
ball-end nylon strings 47
barre chord 76
bass string 64
bottom string 64
bridge 14
bridge pin 14
capo .60
chord diagram 89
chord frame 89
chord grid 89
chord progression 97

chromatic tuners 64
classical guitar 18–19
concert (body size) 33
cutaway 16
D-modal tuning 100
dad gad 100
Dobro 18
double-dropped-D tuning . . .100
dreadnought 33
dropped-D tuning 100
electric guitar 13
endpin 46
extra-hard tension 48
extra-light gauge 48
extra-low tension 48
f-hole 16
fingerboard 14
fingerboard width 35
fingerpicking 58
fingerpicks 58

fingerstyle 58
flamenco guitar 19
flat 67
flatpick 58
flatpicking 58
flattop guitar 13
flight case 54
footstool 46
free stroke 22
fret 14
friction peg 19
gears 63
gig bag 54
golpeador 19
grand auditorium (body size) 33
grand concert (body size) . . .33
gut-string guitar 19
half step 60
hard tension 48
hard-shell case 54
harmonic 68
Hawaiian style 18
headstock 14
heel 14
high E string 64
inlay .14
intonation 36
jumbo 33
laminated wood 29
light gauge 48
low E string 64
low tension 48
lower bout 14
luthier 32
magnetic pickup 15
medium gauge 48
medium-light gauge 48

National 18
neck .14
neck angle 36
neck profile 34
normal tension 48
nut 44
nylon strings 47
nylon-string guitar 18
octaves 67
OM 33
open tuning 99
open-C tuning 100
open-D tuning 100
open-G tuning 100
parlor guitar 33
pick .58
pick and fingers 59
pickguard 14
plectrum 58
position 90
position marker 14
purfling 32
resonator guitar 17
resophonic guitar 17
rest stroke 22
root note 77
rosette 14
saddle 44
scale length 35
setup 43
sharp 67
shim .44
silk-and-steel strings 48
six-on-a-side tuners 15
slotted headstock 51
soft-shell case 54
solid body 15

solid headstock 51

solid wood 29

soundboard 14

soundhole 14

soundhole humidifier 56

square neck 17

standard notation 91

standard tuning 63

steel strings 47

steel-string guitar 13

strap button 46

string gauges 48

string winder 45

Suzuki method 88

tab 90

tablature 90

tailpiece 17

thumbpick 58

tonic .96

top string 64

trapeze tailpiece 16

treble string 64

truss rod 44

tuners 63

tuning fork 65

tuning machine 63

tuning peg 63

unison 68

upper bout 14

vintage 32

waist 14

whammy bar 15

whole step 60

ABOUT THE AUTHOR

Jeffrey Pepper Rodgers has been pursuing his twin passions for words and music since he was a teenager. He became the founding editor of *Acoustic Guitar* in 1990 and led the magazine through its tenth anniversary. These days he continues to write extensively on all aspects of the guitar scene, edits a variety of music-related books, and moderates the beginning guitar forum at www.acousticguitar.com. He is the author of *Rock Troubadours: Conversations on the Art and Craft of Songwriting* (String Letter Publishing), which features his interviews with Paul Simon, Dave Matthews, Jerry Garcia, Joni Mitchell, Ani DiFranco, and others.

As a musician, Rodgers has been writing and playing original songs for more than 20 years. His all-acoustic, home-recorded CD, *Traveling Songs*, can be sampled at www.JeffreyPepperRodgers.com, along with some of his writings about music and other subjects. In addition to singing and playing the guitar, Rodgers has studied North Indian tabla drumming extensively, both in the U.S. and in India.

ACKNOWLEDGMENTS

Many thanks to all the guitarists and teachers who share their sage advice in these pages: Ben Harbert, Jimmy Tomasello, Cathy Fink, Marcy Marxer, Carol McComb, Fred Noad, Jacob Sweet, Margie Mirken, Stan Jay, Bill Purse, Jessica Baron Turner, Stan Werbin, Mark Dvorak, Sonia Michelson, and Paul Kotapish. A special nod to Ben Harbert for hooking me up with the teaching staff at Chicago's Old Town School of Folk Music, a very deep well of knowledge and experience. Equally important was the behind-the-scenes editorial feedback of Richard Johnston, Teja Gerken, Scott Nygaard, Simone Solondz, and Stacey Lynn. And I am honored that Pete Seeger, best friend of beginners everywhere, found the time to review my manuscript.

Last but not least, the denizens of *Acoustic Guitar*'s beginner forum offered insightful questions as well as answers that helped shape this book—giving each other incredible support along the way.

I'd like to dedicate the *Beginning Guitarist's Handbook* to Lila, who is excitedly learning her first chords as this book goes to press.